IMAGES
of America

HEADWATERS PARK

FORT WAYNE'S LASTING LEGACY

IMAGES
of America

HEADWATERS PARK

FORT WAYNE'S LASTING LEGACY

Geoff Paddock

ARCADIA
PUBLISHING

Published by Arcadia Publishing
Charleston, South Carolina

Library of Congress Catalog Card Number: 2002103785

For all general information contact Arcadia Publishing at:
Telephone 843-853-2070
Fax 843-853-0044
E-Mail sales@arcadiapublishing.com
For customer service and orders:
Toll-Free 1-888-313-2665

Visit us on the Internet at www.arcadiapublishing.com

To Kathleen and Stephen Paddock and Carl Offerle

CONTENTS

ACKNOWLEDGMENTS

I would like to acknowledge the following people and organizations:

Randy Elliot
Tom Castaldi
Ralph Violette
John Beatty
Central Soya Company
Gabe Delobbe
Allen County Fort Wayne Historical Society
Allen County Public Library
Headwaters Park Commission
Headwaters Park Alliance
State of Indiana
City of Fort Wayne
Fort Wayne Bicentennial Commission
Eric R. Kuhne and Associates
Grinsfelder Associates Architects
LandPlan Group
Brooks Construction Company
Hamilton Hunter Builders
Leeper's Lawn Service
Robin and Mike Holley
Susan Meiser

INTRODUCTION

The Headwaters Flood Control and Park Project is an environmentally sound addition to the Fort Wayne area, bringing several important goals together. Among these goals are flood mitigation, economic development, recreation, and outdoor education.

The first and most important aspect of the Headwaters project is to curb the flooding problem and the damage it causes to the citizens of Fort Wayne. The park's natural construction will actually aid in the free flowing of the Saint Mary's River. Because structures are no longer located in the thumb area of the park, they do not act as an impediment to the flowing of the flood waters. Therefore, Headwaters Park should actually decrease some of the devastating effects caused by recent flooding. Because businesses will no longer be located in this flood prone area, the damage to the city's economy will be much less severe after a flood is experienced. In 1985, the damage in the thumb alone was estimated to be $3.9 million — more than half the total damage estimated for the entire community. Flood damage to the area from the floods of 1978, 1982, and 1991 amounted to over $10 million.

Another goal of the project is to enhance the overall economic development efforts of the community. Headwaters has become home to such annual festivals as Germanfest, the Three Rivers Festival, and many others. The park provides use to thousands of people and has become a focal point for festivals and other events. In 2001, twelve festivals joined almost 20 other not-for-profit, business, and children's events in finding a home in the park

A third important aspect of the park is to connect the downtown area with the Rivergreenway. Headwaters serves as an intermediary point along the Rivergreenway, which consists of a series of parks and trails along the rivers of Fort Wayne. Educational opportunities, especially for our area's young people, abound in the park. They can spend time learning about and identifying various kinds of trees, flowers, and native Indiana grasses near the Great Meadow, as fog misters shoot from the top of a 21st century pavilion and from around the gardens. At the same time, they can learn about an environmentally conscious way of dealing with flood waters. During festival season from May until October, young people can experience various kinds of languages, dance interpretation, craft design, and other applications of the arts. On hot summer days, they can refresh in the two large, interactive water fountains.

Headwaters Park is bringing more people to downtown Fort Wayne. It attracts citizens to the city from all parts of northeast Indiana and northwest Ohio and serves as a welcome addition to the economic development efforts of the Fort Wayne area.

The architectural plan, as developed by Eric R. Kuhne and Associates and implemented by Grinsfelder Associates, took years to develop and perfect. The architects determined this plan would best serve the ultimate use of a park located in a flood plain. It was only after careful study and public input that this plan was adopted by the Headwaters Park Commission.

In the late 1990s, Headwaters Park became one of the largest public-private partnerships existing in Northern Indiana. Together, both the public and private sectors raised nearly $17 million to complete the downtown revitalization. Because of its broad appeal, support came from all areas of the community. The State of Indiana contributed $2 million, mostly through Build Indiana funds for land acquisition. Fort Wayne and Allen County governments contributed $5.2 million for land acquisition, environmental remediation, and business relocation costs. The Headwaters Park Commission raised just over $9.7 million from private sources and secured $850,000 of this as a partial maintenance and operating endowment. Over 2,000 citizens had their names engraved on walkway bricks. Others purchased park benches, lamp posts, or one of over 600 trees added to the downtown landscape.

Headwaters Park was endorsed by the Isaac Walton League, business and labor groups, the Fort Wayne Chamber of Commerce, and the Convention and Visitor's Bureau. It is a lasting legacy to the city that saved itself from devastating flooding and was dedicated on October 22, 1999, the city's 205th birthday. Truly, this project has united our community and will serve it a century from now.

Geoff Paddock, Executive Director, Headwaters Park Alliance
March 2002

THE HEADWATERS PARK ALLIANCE

Eleanor H. Marine, President
Marty Bender
Tim Borne
Madelane Elston
Christopher Guerin
Kathy Harvard
Sandra Kennedy
Jan Paflas
Suzon Motz
Molly McCray
Ian Rolland
Charles Redd
John Shoaff
David Steiner
Judy Zehner

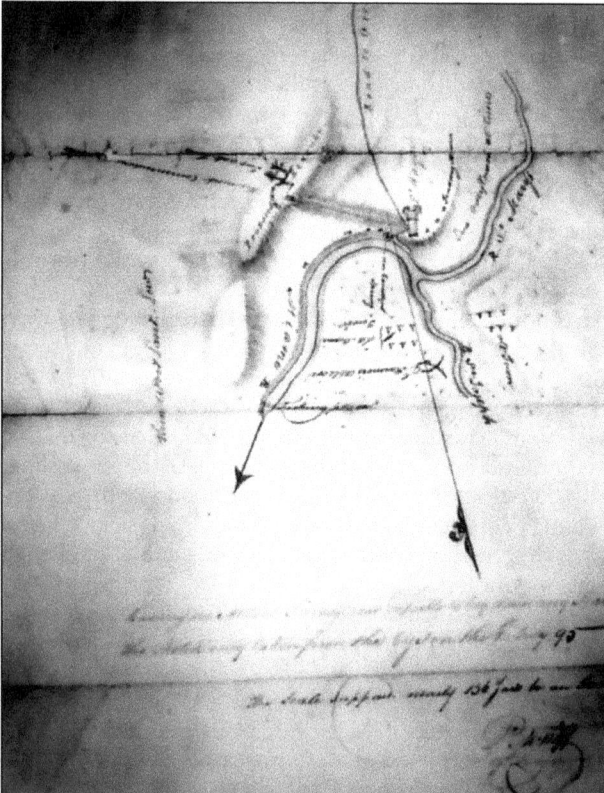

This drawing depicts the encampment of General Anthony Wayne near the confluence of the three rivers in the mid 1790s. Wayne's original fort was south and east of Headwaters Park in higher ground on what is now the corner of Berry and Clay Streets. The fort was originally dedicated on October 22, 1794, which became the official founding day of the city. (Allen County/Fort Wayne Historical Society.)

One

THE EARLY YEARS

The story of the Headwaters Flood Control and Park Project begins at the earliest recorded time, when glaciers covered most of the Fort Wayne area. The glaciers melted some 10,000 years ago, and the three rivers were created. Early native people were able to live in the area, finding game and vegetation to survive. The St. Mary's and St. Joseph Rivers met to form the headwaters of the Maumee, which flowed east to Lake Erie. To the west is the Continental Divide, where the waters flow into the Wabash River and eventually to the Gulf of Mexico.

Created near this confluence of the three rivers, was a thumb-shaped land that was wet and marshy much of the time. Native Americans and early settlers were wise not to inhabit this flood prone area. In the late 1600s, Native Americans and some Europeans settled in higher ground south of the confluence, since this area was a portage between the Maumee and the Wabash Rivers. This land was the shortest water route between the Great Lakes and the Gulf of Mexico, so French trappers also made their way here.

Humans declined to settle in the thumb, which was under water during heavy spring rain showers. The first recorded flood inundated the land in 1790. The subsequent floods Fort Wayne experienced from the eighteenth century to the twenty-first century, demonstrated why development of permanent settlements in the flood plain is unwise.

A French fort was built west of Headwaters Park in 1722. The French had established themselves in this area since the late 1600's, and sought to command the important portage that connected the Maumee and Wabash Rivers. Fur trading with Native Americans flourished and rare beaver and deerskin pelts were exported to France and other parts of Europe. Later in the 1700s, four additional forts were erected, but on higher ground. The French surrendered their fort to the British, but the Revolutionary War securely placed this land in the hands of the Americans. In 1794, General Anthony Wayne was commissioned to build a fort here. On October 22, 1794, Fort Wayne was dedicated, built on high ground and overlooking the confluence of the three rivers.

Prior to white settlers coming to Fort Wayne, the Miami Indian people dominated the land. Me-she-kin-no-quah, known to Euro-Americans as "Little Turtle," was born in 1747. He played a significant role in the settlement of the land surrounding the confluence. Little Turtle fought many successful wars against the onslaught of white settlers in the late 1700s. He was a gallant warrior who defeated many armies, including those led by General Josiah Harmar and General Arthur St. Clair. President George Washington worried about Little Turtle and his prominence in the Midwest. He sent General Anthony Wayne to conquer the Native American leaders and make peace in the region. This occurred with the Treaty of Greenville in 1795. Little Turtle appeared as gracious in defeat as he had been in victory. He later visited President Washington and Presidents John Adams and Thomas Jefferson. He died in 1812 and was buried in higher ground about one mile north and east of Headwaters Park.

When glaciers of the great Ice Age melted some 10,000 years ago, the Maumee Terrain was formed as the result in Northeastern Indiana. It is here that three rivers met; the Saint Joseph and the Saint Mary's, formed the headwaters of the Maumee River, which flows in a northeasterly direction towards Lake Erie. Fort Wayne became the site of a portage to the Wabash, Ohio, and Mississippi Rivers. A plaque in Headwaters Park, dedicated on October 22, 1999, documents the first Americans to settle in this new land. (Glacier photograph courtesy of Allen County/Fort Wayne Historical Society. Plaque photograph courtesy of Headwaters Park Alliance, Inc.)

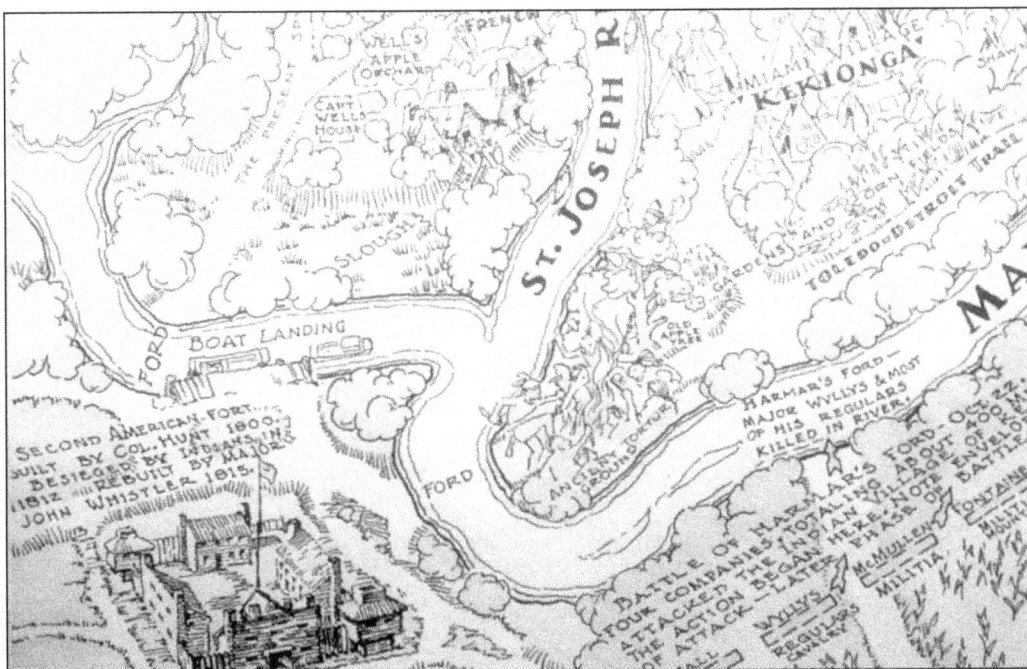

These drawings of Fort Wayne and the confluence of the three rivers depict a settlement beginning to grow in the early 1800s. The official map of Fort Wayne, shown here in about 1812, highlights the prominence of the three rivers in the development of the settlement. The thumb of the Saint Mary's River is located in the center of the map. It would later become the site of Headwaters Park. (AC/FW Historical Society.)

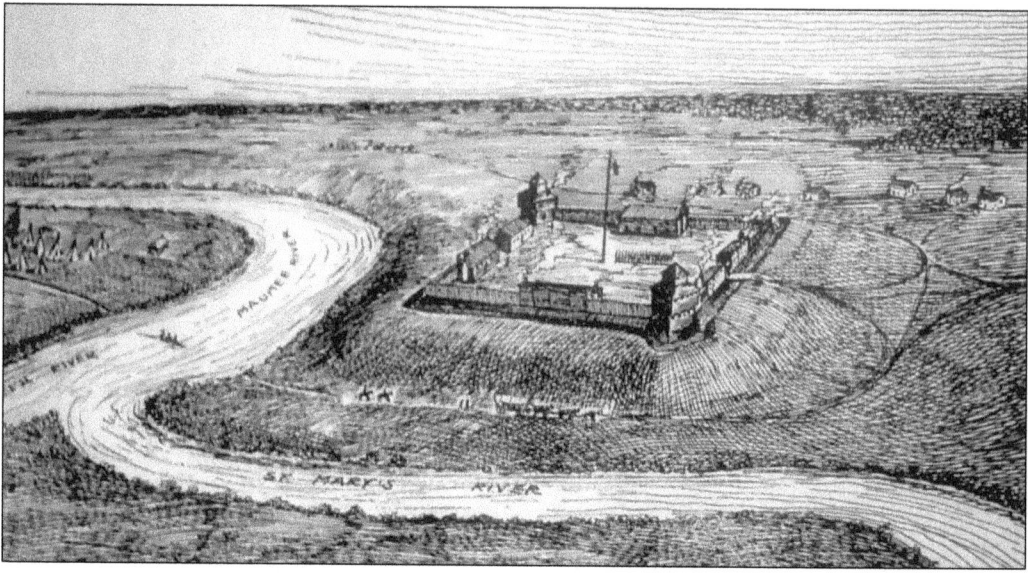

Above, below, and opposite are views of the early settlement depicting a small village beginning to spring up outside the stockade and near the rivers.

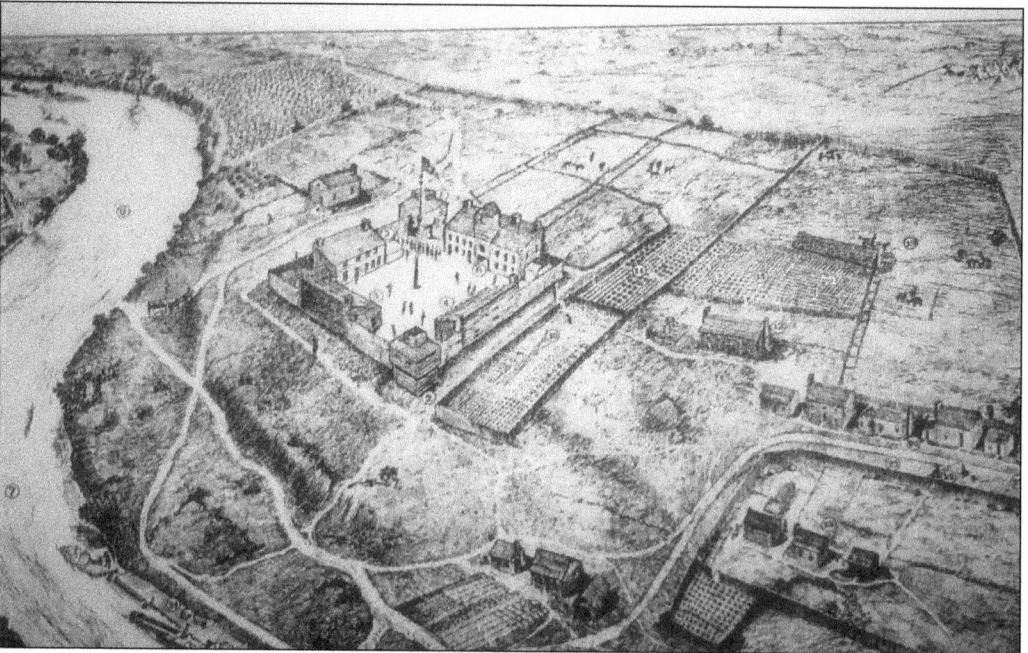

The image above is perhaps the most famous of the three engravings, the conception by Dr. Charles E. Slocum, author of the history of the Maumee River Basin. Dr. Slocum spent time in Fort Wayne making surveys to determine the location of the fort and the contour of the land at the time of General Anthony Wayne. (AC/FW Historical Society.)

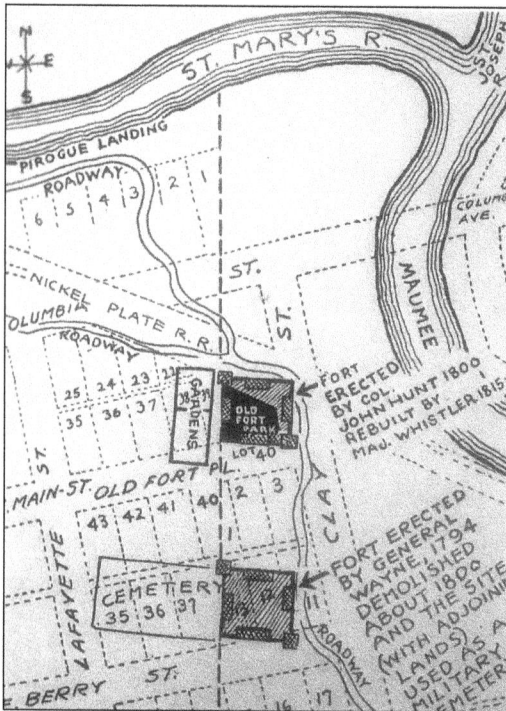

This map of early Fort Wayne shows the original stockade just south of the fort built by General Anthony Wayne in 1794, erected by Col. John Hunt in 1800, and rebuilt by Major John Whistler in 1815 and 1816. The Anthony Wayne fort was located on ground now occupied by the Cinema Center and Hall Art Center. The Hunt/Whistler fort was located at the present site of the central Fire Station on Main Street. Both of these stockades were constructed on higher ground than the replica fort of 1976, which is located near the confluence of the three rivers and just to the east of Headwaters Park. (AC/FW Historical Society.)

Little Turtle, also known as Mishikinakwa, was chief of the Miami Nation in the late 1700s and early 1800s. He was one of the most successful Native American resistance leaders during this time. He defeated armies led by Generals Harmer and Saint Clair but was no match for Anthony Wayne, who defeated him in 1794. Little Turtle later made peace with Wayne and his followers and played a significant role in the settlement around the confluence, which would later become part of Headwaters Park. (AC/FW Historical Society.)

14

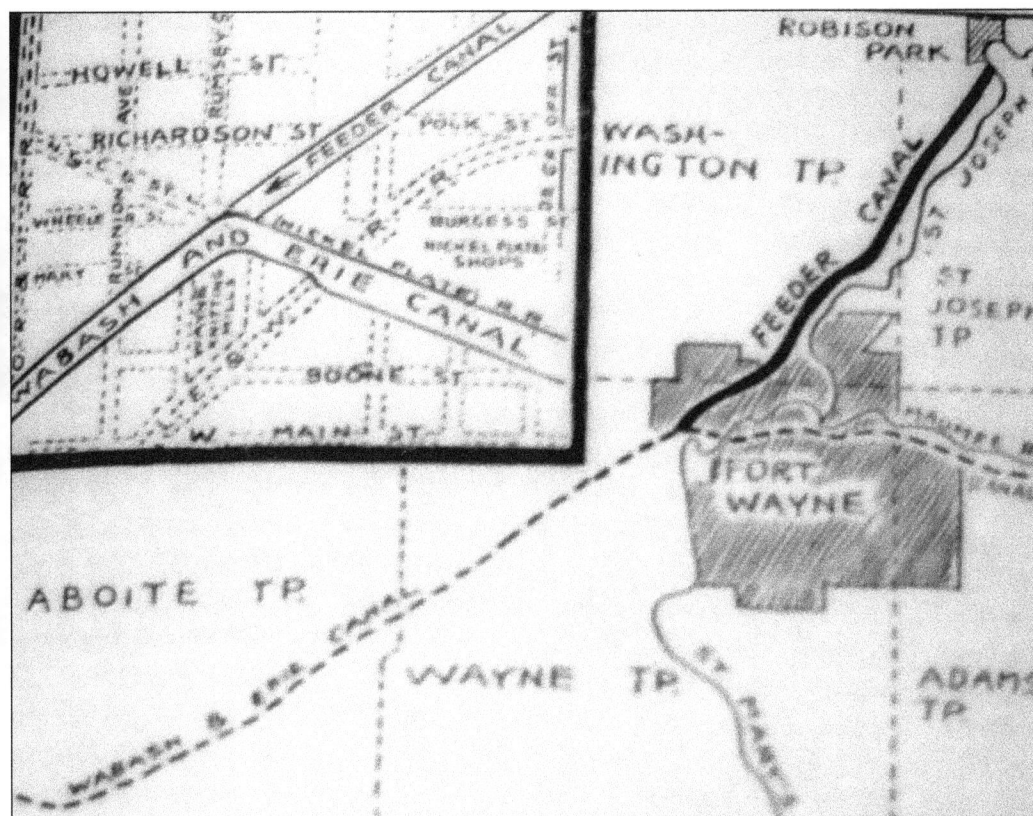

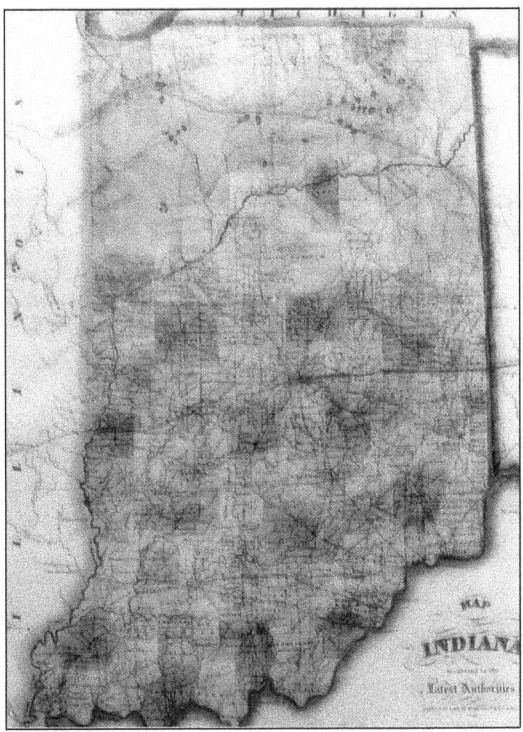

These two maps show the growth of Indiana around 1820 and the emergence of the Wabash and Erie Canal. The canal, which is depicted by the dotted line, was vital to the growth of Fort Wayne. It was constructed in the 1830s and 40s and cut across the city just south of the thumb and the confluence of the three rivers, which were not navigable. The thumb is the site of Headwaters Park, constructed a century and a half after the completion of the canal. (AC/FW Historical Society.)

This 19th-century painting depicts cattle wading; it was believed to be published in Harper's Weekly Magazine in the early 1850s. The area in the background is now the Lakeside area, formerly known as the Apple Orchard. (Eric R. Kuhne and Associates, New York.)

Two

GROWTH IN
THE 19TH CENTURY

Ground was broken for the Wabash-Erie Canal on February 22, 1832. The canal proved important to the growth of the city and the western portion of the United States. The first leg, linking Fort Wayne to Lafayette, was completed on July 4, 1843 and anchored the south end of Headwaters Park. By 1853, the Wabash-Erie Canal was 468 miles in length and was the longest canal in the western hemisphere, connecting the Saint Lawrence Seaway and the Gulf of Mexico. Improved transportation led to commercial and agricultural developments, and Fort Wayne and other towns along the canal's path flourished.

As America grew in the 1850s and 1860s, the popularity of the railroad also grew. Eventually, the Wabash-Erie Canal became obsolete, and it was filled in to make way for a new railway connecting many cities in the Midwest. Purchasing the right-of-way of the old canal allowed officials from the New York, Chicago, & Saint Louis Railroad, also known as the Nickel Plate Road, to build a railroad through a Midwestern city without having to raze one building. The new railroad also came within two blocks of the new courthouse. The railroad was elevated in 1955, allowing the north side of Fort Wayne to grow. This elevation is an historic landmark structure on the south border of Headwaters Park.

The canal and railroads brought commerce to Fort Wayne. Even though the thumb had been known for years as a marsh and swamp, efforts were made to fill in the land and bring industry of the 1800s to central Fort Wayne. By the mid 1850s, grain and lumber mills, blacksmiths, and brick and tile makers, dotted the landscape of what is now the southern portion of Headwaters Park. The circus set up temporary tents in the northern half of the thumb, when dry weather was prevalent. The "Birdboy of Fort Wayne," Art Smith, practiced takeoffs and landings in his new plane in the early 1900s. In the late 1920s, the National Guard Armory was completed on the west side of Clinton Street that now spanned the Saint Mary's River. Perhaps the most famous structure to grace this section of town was League Park. Professional, organized league baseball teams played there beginning in 1871. One of the first lighted baseball games was played there in 1880. Babe Ruth supposedly hit a home run while playing at League Park in the minor leagues in 1927. All of this development occurred despite the ongoing flooding from the river.

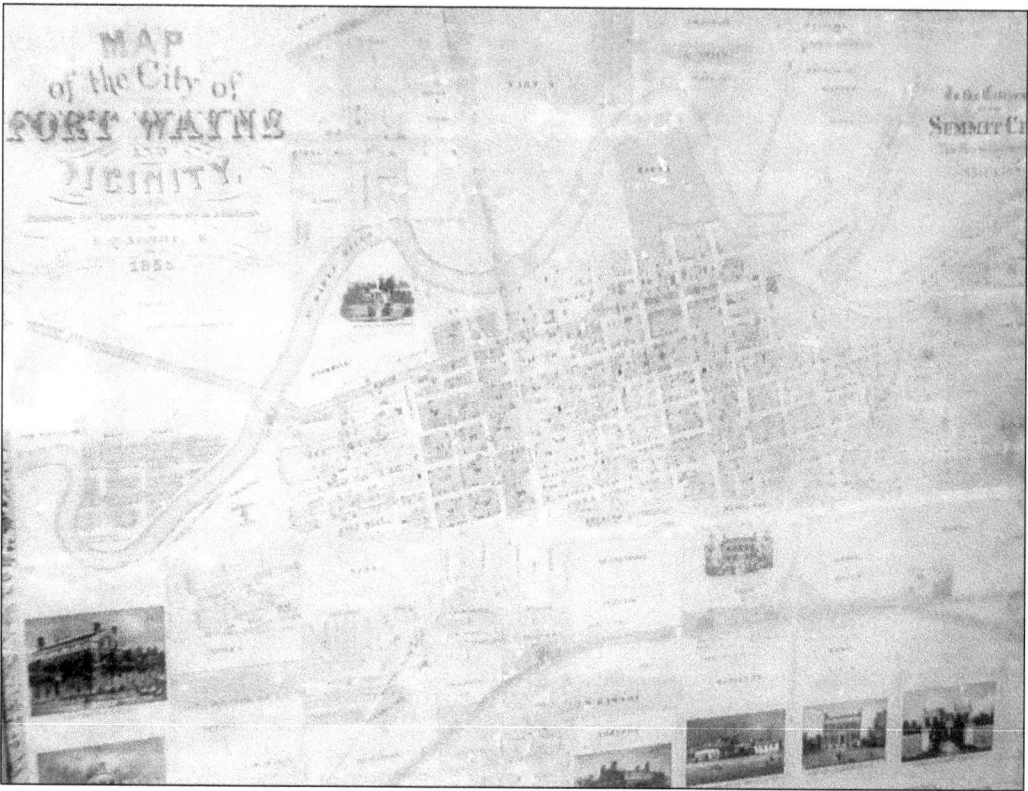

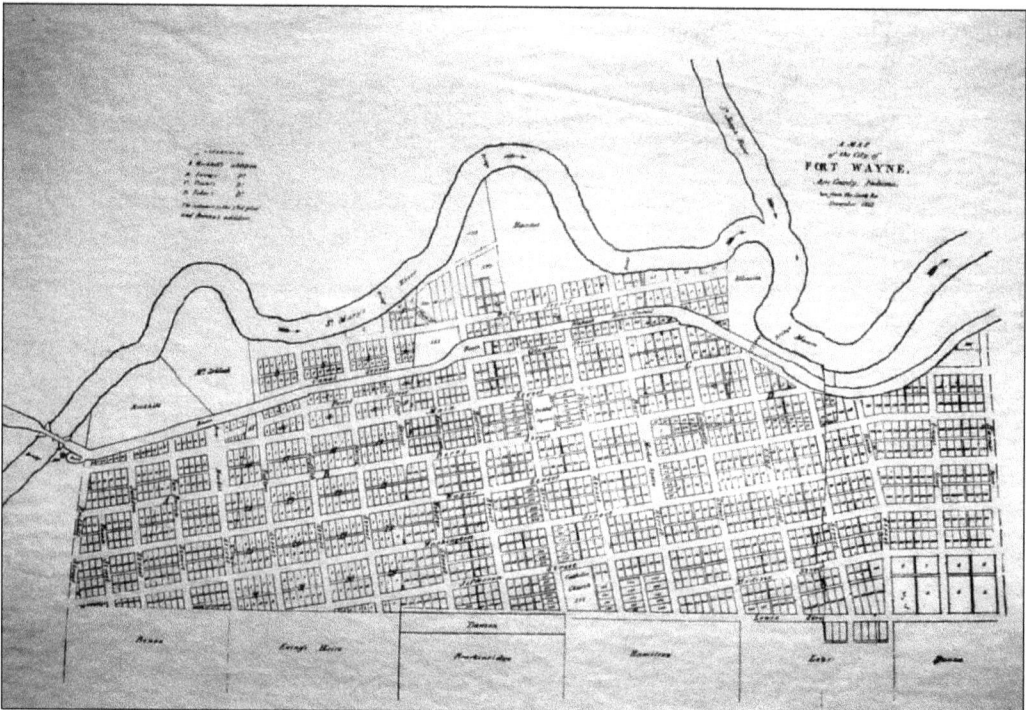

18

Early maps of Fort Wayne chart the growth of the community and the prominence of the Wabash and Erie Canal in the development of the city. The canal was constructed through the heart of the city in the 1830s and 40s. The canal provided the south anchor to the large plot of ground that later became Headwaters Park. The arched tip of land, later identified as the thumb, is visible from these maps of the 1850s and 60s. While the city grew south of the canal, little development occurred north of the thumb until the early 1900s. (AC/FW Historical Society.)

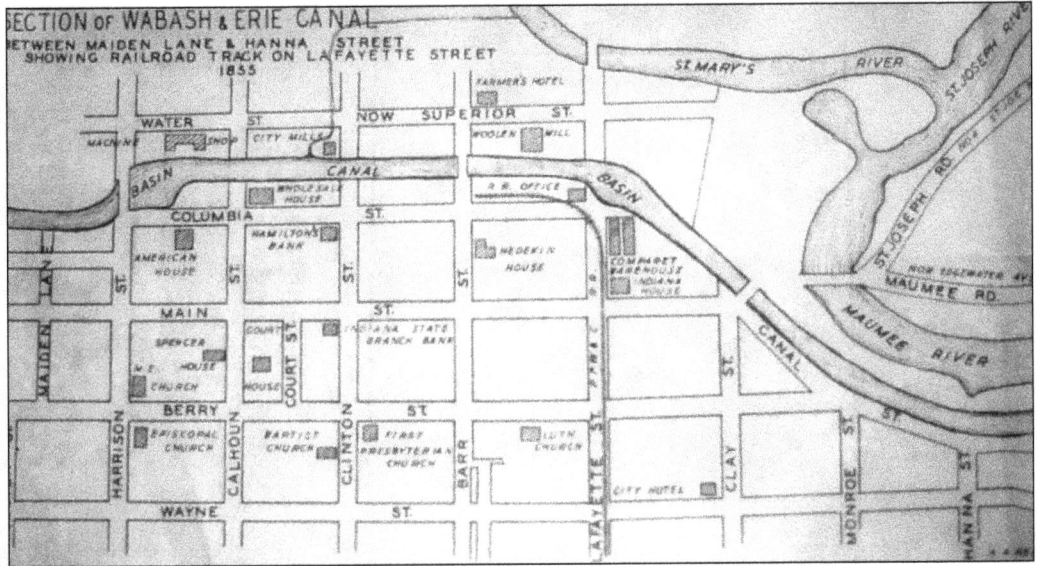

Two interpretations of the canal meeting and crossing the Saint Mary's River just blocks west of the downtown area and the thumb are known as the Wabash and Erie Canal Aqueduct. The drawing is from Griswold's book, *The Pictoral History of Fort Wayne*, and the painting hangs in the Historical Museum. Both are circa 1840. The canal made possible continuous water traffic between the Saint Lawrence Seaway and the Gulf of Mexico. (AC/FW Historical Society.)

This drawing from a woodcut in Lossing's Pictorial Fieldbook of the War of 1812, shows a wooden bridge crossing the Maumee River just south of the confluence and just east of the thumb. The site is now the Columbia Street bridge as it crosses from the Lakeside area and enters downtown Fort Wayne. (AC/FW Historical Society.)

The importance of the Wabash and Erie Canal in the development and growth of Fort Wayne again is depicted in the above painting of the canal in use. One of the last remaining canal houses of the late 19th century was converted into a textile retail shop and later into a popular restaurant, Club Soda, anchoring the south border of Headwaters Park. Its importance as a trading station was diminished when the railroad came to town. (AC/FW Historical Society.)

A section of the canal is shown here in ruins on a cold snowy day in the late 1800s. The canal was soon to be filled in and a railroad built in its place as the mode of transportation evolved from water to rail. The Nickel Plate Railroad, also known as the New York, Chicago, and Saint Louis Railroad, was constructed over the canal bed in 1881. It passed two blocks from the Courthouse and just to the south of the thumb of Headwaters Park. (AC/FW Historical Society.)

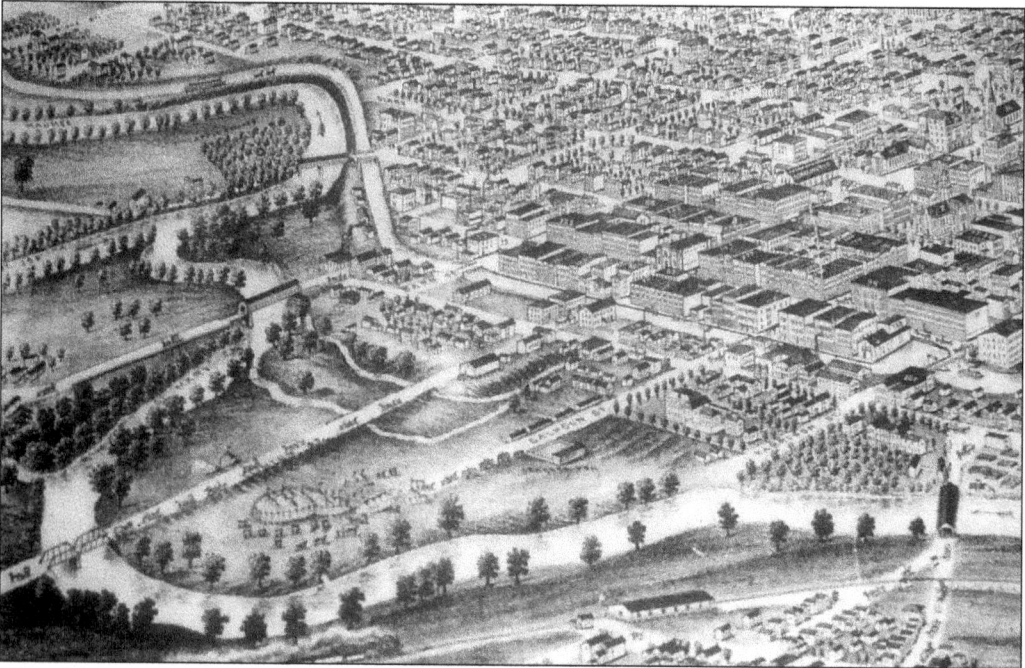

This depiction of Fort Wayne, prominently featuring the thumb, was produced in 1868. The drawing shows the growth of the city to the south. The thumb is basically at the northern tip of the city, although some growth has occurred north of the river. The thumb was not commercially developed at this time but served—when not flooded—as a home for the circus, as the tent depicts. (AC/FW Historical Society.)

22

Here is another angle of the 1868 bird's-eye view of the city which shows covered bridges spanning the rivers and the prominence of the thumb at the north end of Fort Wayne. The Wabash and Erie Canal is clearly visible as it winds through the northern edge of town and just south of the thumb. (AC/FW Historical Society.)

A bustling scene of downtown Fort Wayne is shown in this picture taken in 1889. It is the intersection of Main and Calhoun Streets, the heart of downtown. Looking north on Calhoun Street, a trolley car appears to be making its way north, eventually ending its service as Calhoun Street terminates in the thumb. (AC Public Library.)

By the late 1890s, the Wagner Drug Store was located on the corner of Main and Calhoun Streets just south of the thumb. (AC Public Library.)

Until the 1880s, public hangings were a common site in Fort Wayne, just north of the jail flats. The last public hanging is shown in this drawing of Sam McDonald being hung in 1883. He was accused of killing Louis Laurent and was hanged before a crowd of 250 in what is now Phase IV of Headwaters Park. (AC/FW Historical Society.)

Three

DEVELOPMENT IN THE 20TH CENTURY

Despite many successful enterprises constructed in the thumb in the 1800s and 1900s, some of the activity that occurred there was despicable and unwanted. The site was known as the jail flats, and Allen County's first jail was constructed there in 1849. This became a place for public hangings, the last one occurring in 1883. It was also a site where many prisoners escaped over the years. In 1913, League Park was badly damaged in a fire, and the structure was totally destroyed by fire in 1930. The 1930s also saw the rise of shantytowns and "Hoovervilles" all over the country. The most prominent one in Fort Wayne was located in Headwaters Park. The thumb was filled with tar paper shacks, traveling "hobos," and misery, as homeless people tried to live through the Great Depression. As the economy improved, the shantytown was torn down. By 1939, all existing buildings were razed.

Economic activity of the 1940s and 1950s led to the rebirth of the thumb with the widening of Clinton Street and the elevation of the railroad. More fill had been brought in over the years, and Headwaters Park was now dotted with service stations, car dealers, and retail businesses. By 1960, nearly all of the thirty acres composing the thumb hosted a business or parking lot to serve downtown Fort Wayne. All the concrete and asphalt melded in this area did nothing to help drain excess water from the Saint Mary's River. Often businesses and industry were devastated by flood waters—but they always came back. Downtown was thriving and every square foot of retail business space was valuable, even the thirty acres in the flood plain.

Fort Wayne is built around three rivers, and most often these waterways brought prosperity to the city. People settled here in part because of the rivers and because the city was in the center of a portage between the Wabash River system and the Maumee River. The city grew in the nineteenth century and became inundated with concrete and asphalt. This prevented adequate drainage, and Fort Wayne experienced flooding. The Great Flood of 1913 saw the Maumee rise overnight from seven feet to twenty-six feet. Fifteen thousand people fled their homes and six people died. After the disaster, the city built a series of flood protection walls around several neighborhoods. More floods occurred in the 1920s, 30s, and 40s and devastating floods once again occurred in 1978, 1982, 1985, and 1991, causing millions of dollars of damage to residential property, businesses, and inventory. After each flood, the city was rebuilt, causing it to be dubbed the "City That Saved Itself."

These pictures show further development of the city in the early 1900s. These two buildings, one a business on Harrison Street, and the other a home on Eureka Street, depict life in the early 20th century. Eureka Street was later to become Clair Street and part of the development of the park. (AC/FW Historical Society.)

THE FLOOD OF 1913

The following pictures (through page 35) depict the devastation of the great Flood of 1913, the so-called "100 year flood" that occurred several times in the 20th century. This photograph shows homes along Eureka Street facing the river and built on stilts to avoid flood damage. The scene is the Saint Mary's River as it creeps higher in March of 1913, just beyond the Harrison Street Bridge. The area now is part of the greenway connection and parking area for Headwaters Park.

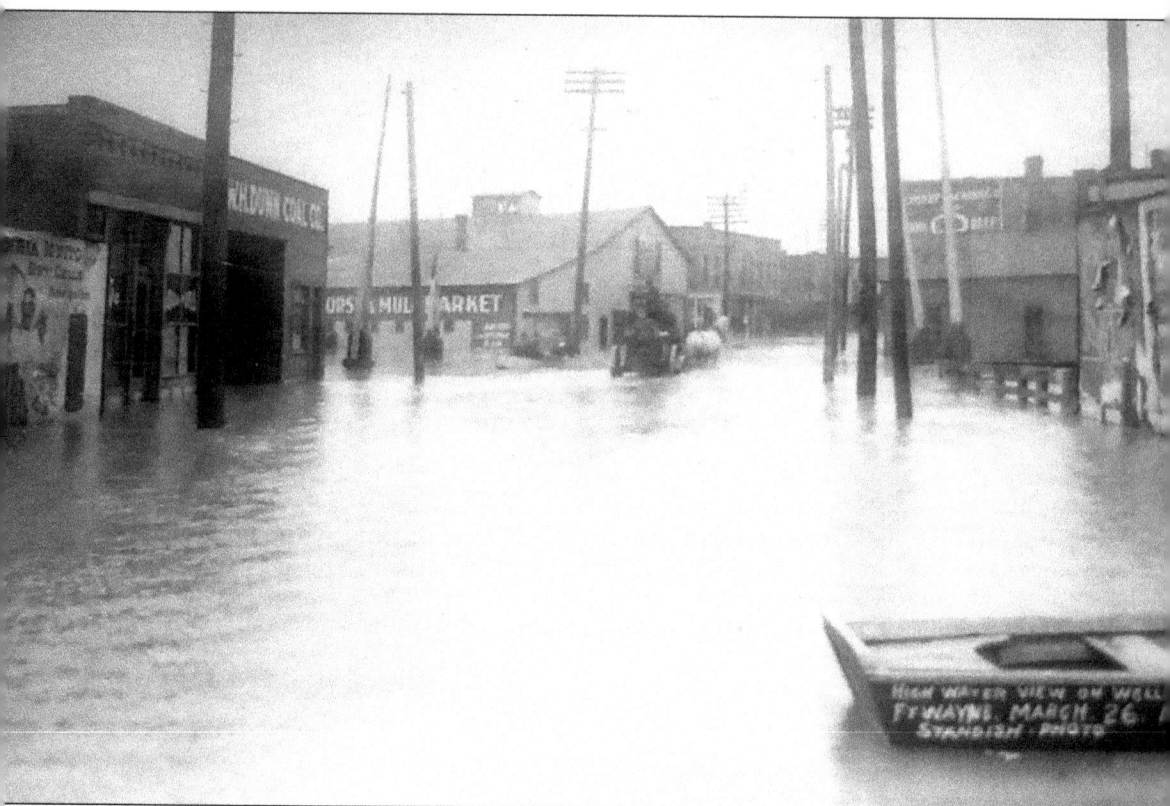

A flooded Wells Street, just north and east of the thumb, on March 26, 1913. Six people were killed as a result of the flooding, and Fort Wayne began to change the way it built itself around the three rivers. (AC/FW Historical Society.)

Water covers Spy Run Avenue (later Highway 27) leading north near the intersection of Fourth Street, northwest of the thumb. This picture was taken on March 25, 1913. (AC/FW Historical Society.)

The famous Columbia Street Bridge, pictured earlier in a drawing from 1812, is seen just above the flood waters and south of the confluence of the three rivers. (AC/FW Historical Society.)

Shown here is Clinton Street, just north of the thumb and near the intersection of Fourth Street, in March of 1913. A rowboat stands ready to traverse the flooded street. Sandbags can be seen in the upper right of the photograph. (AC/FW Historical Society.)

Superior Street, crosses just to the south of the thumb, looks west from the Flood of 1913. (AC/ FW Historical Society.)

Homes along Calhoun Street face the Saint Mary's River as it rises in March of 1913. Clothes can be seen hanging on the back porch to dry. (AC/FW Historical Society.)

This photograph is believed to be another flooded home located on Superior Street near the thumb. (AC Public Library)

The images on this page and opposite show the baseball stadium peaking out from under water. The stadium would become famous in the 1920s for hosting exhibition games with baseball greats such as Babe Ruth, Bobby Matthews, and Zane Grey . In 1913, the Fort Wayne Baseball Park withstood the surging waters of the Saint Mary's River in what is now Headwaters Park.

Flooded Clinton Street, lined with downtown homes and businesses, is located just to the east of the stadium. (AC/FW Historical Society.)

The Great Flood of 1913 is the worst flood on record in Fort Wayne. On March 26, 1913, the Maumee River rose overnight from 7 feet to over 26 feet. Fifteen thousand people were made homeless and six lost their lives. Mayor Jesse Grice organized a heroic relief effort, and martial law was declared, with orders to shoot looters. (AC/FW Historical Society.)

As the water receded, the city water levels returned to normal. This photograph is a shot of the confluence shortly after the Great Flood of 1913. (AC Public Library.)

GREAT FORT WAYNE CENTENNIAL OF JUNE 5 TO 10, 1916

This Birdseye View of the Features of the Celebration and the Heart of the City of Fort Wayne is presented with the Compliments of the

LINCOLN NATIONAL LIFE INSURANCE COMPANY   Home Office, FORT WAYNE, IND.

Just three years later, in 1916, the city had recovered enough to celebrate the State of Indiana's Centennial with a grand industrial exposition in the thumb, just south of the Saint Mary's River. (AC/FW Historical Society.)

In this photograph, c.1920, the city is beginning to expand northward. This is Wells Street, just north of the bridge, which still stands as a connection to the river greenway and an entrance into Headwaters Park. (AC Public Library.)

In the late 1920s, Wells Street experienced much growth west of the thumb (AC Public Library.)

This picture shows the intersection of Wells and Superior Streets in the late 1920s, just south and west of the thumb. (AC Public Library.)

Fort Wayne's rich history of baseball is evident from this photograph of League Park in what is believed to be the late 1920s. League Park was located in what is now Phase I, or the western portion of the thumb, of Headwaters Park. The stadium was damaged by the Flood of 1913, but survived. It was destroyed by fire in 1930. (AC/FW Historical Society.)

One of the great baseball players to utilize League Park was Bobby Matthews, believed to be one of the first players to use the curve ball and spit ball. He played for the Fort Wayne Kekiongas, beginning in about 1870. He was later inducted into the baseball Hall of Fame. (*Fort Wayne Journal Gazette*, August 21, 1949.)

This picture of Babe Ruth was taken at League Park in May of 1927. The New York Yankees played an exhibition game against a home team from Lincoln Life. The game was tied until the tenth inning when Ruth knocked a home run over the right-field fence. Legend has it that it was Ruth's "longest" home run, as the ball traveled over the park's right field fence and into a passing Nickel Plate freight train, rumbling by the tracks along Superior Street. (AC/FW Historical Society.)

This picture from the Fort Wayne Journal Gazette on May 9, 1954 shows another baseball team named the Crestos that claimed a city championship in League Park in 1920. (*Journal Gazette.*)

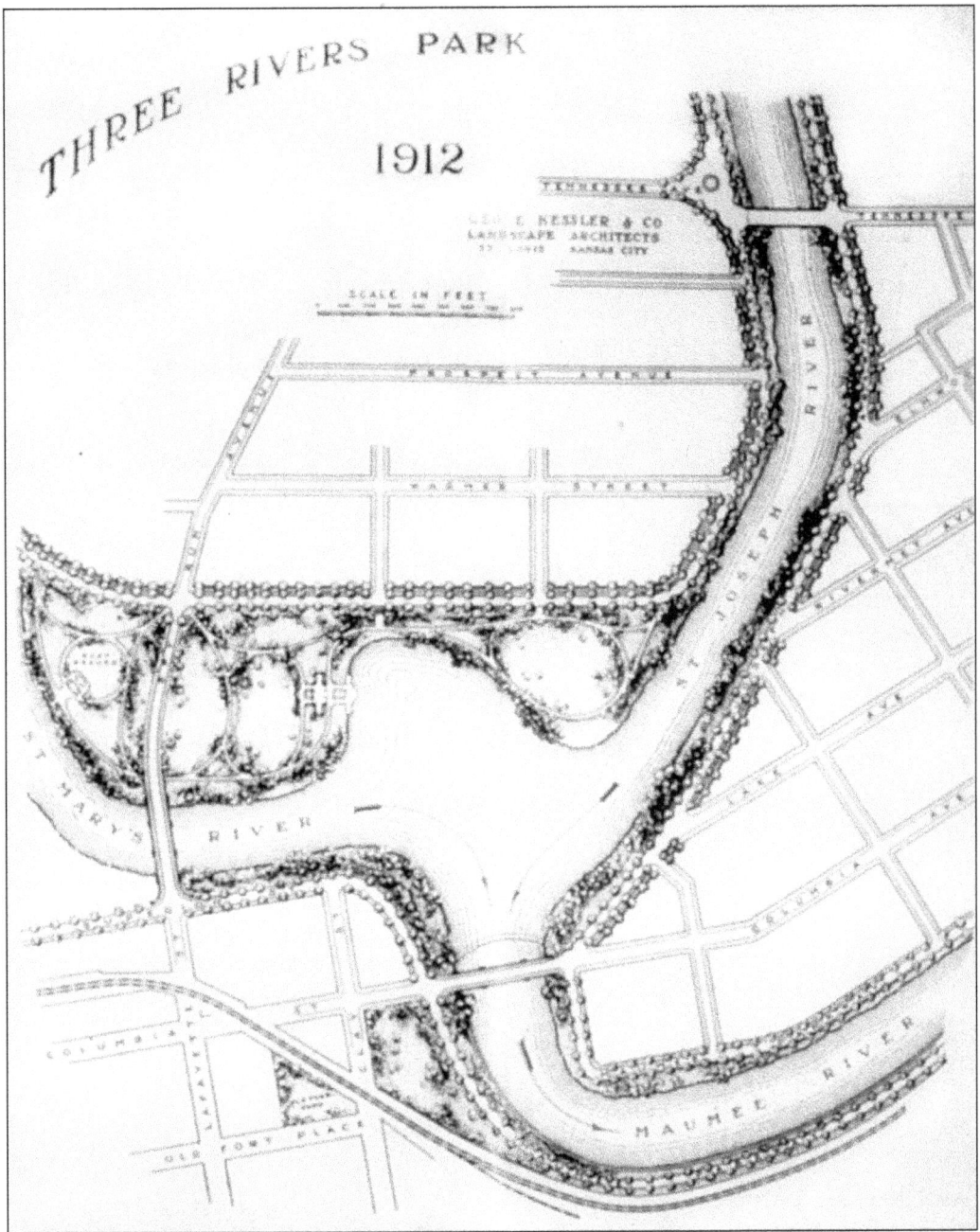

The first recorded plan for a downtown park incorporating the thumb was drawn by nationally known landscape architect George Kessler in 1912. Kessler wanted to reclaim the natural beauty of the city's rivers and create a sweeping plan of riverside drives and parks into the heart of the city. His "Three Rivers Park" was presented to the city's Park Board just days before the March 1913 flood. (AC/FW Historical Society.)

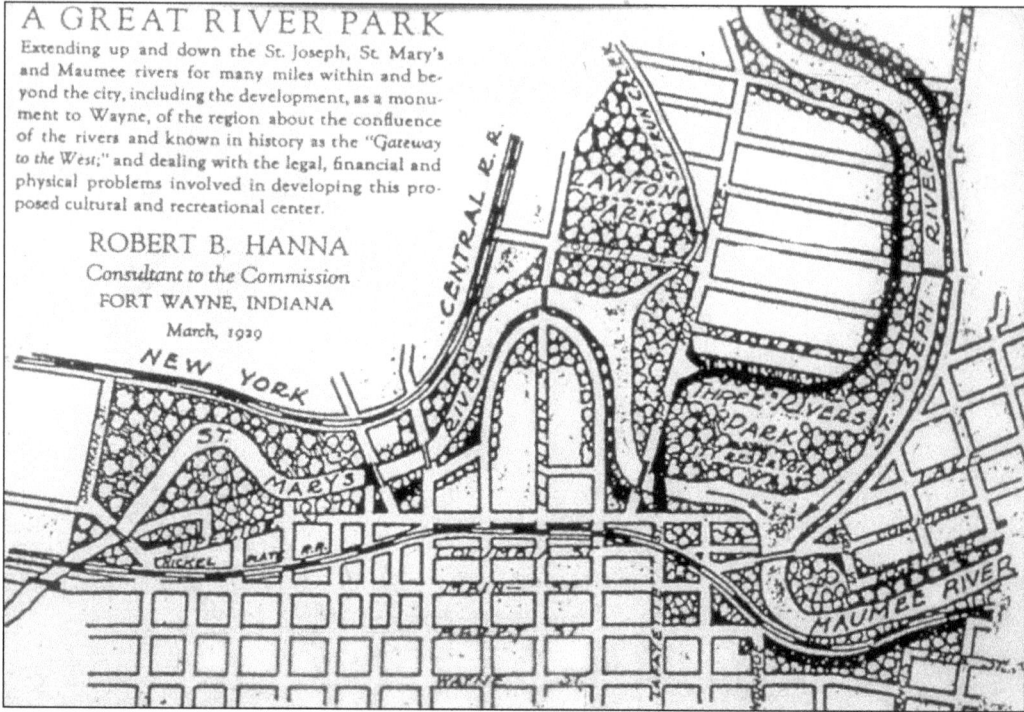

A GREAT RIVER PARK

Extending up and down the St. Joseph, St. Mary's and Maumee rivers for many miles within and beyond the city, including the development, as a monument to Wayne, of the region about the confluence of the rivers and known in history as the "*Gateway to the West*;" and dealing with the legal, financial and physical problems involved in developing this proposed cultural and recreational center.

ROBERT B. HANNA

Consultant to the Commission
FORT WAYNE, INDIANA
March, 1929

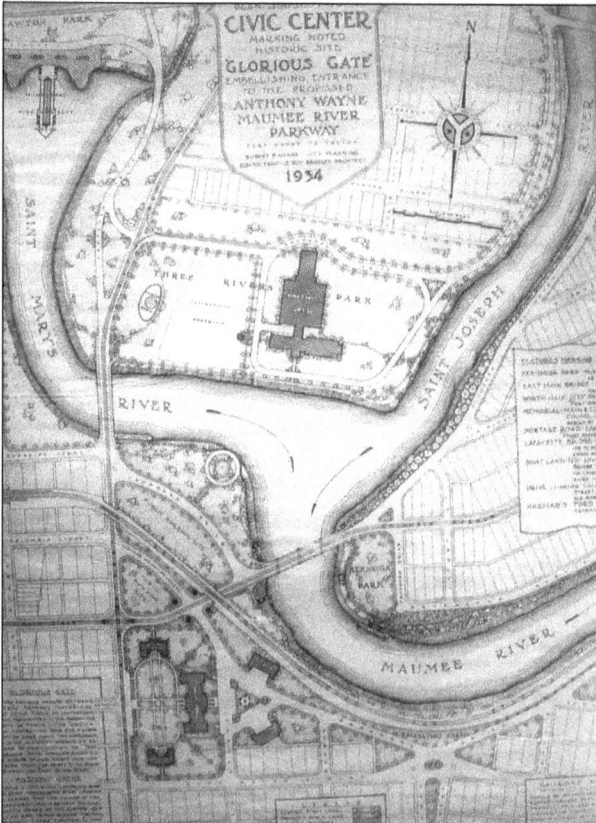

The devastation of the flood and World War I delayed serious consideration of Kessler's plan. In 1929, Robert B. Hanna, a consultant to the City Plan Commission, published a vision for "A Great River Park," which would extend up and down the rivers. Central to his vision was the scenic landscaping of a downtown central park, located in the city's thumb. (AC/FW Historical Society.)

Hanna's plan is shown in this 1934 display at the confluence of the three rivers, bringing forth Kessler's Three Rivers Park theme. Hanna was particularly interested in developing park land around the junction of the rivers, known in history as the "Gateway to the West." (AC/FW Historical Society.)

40

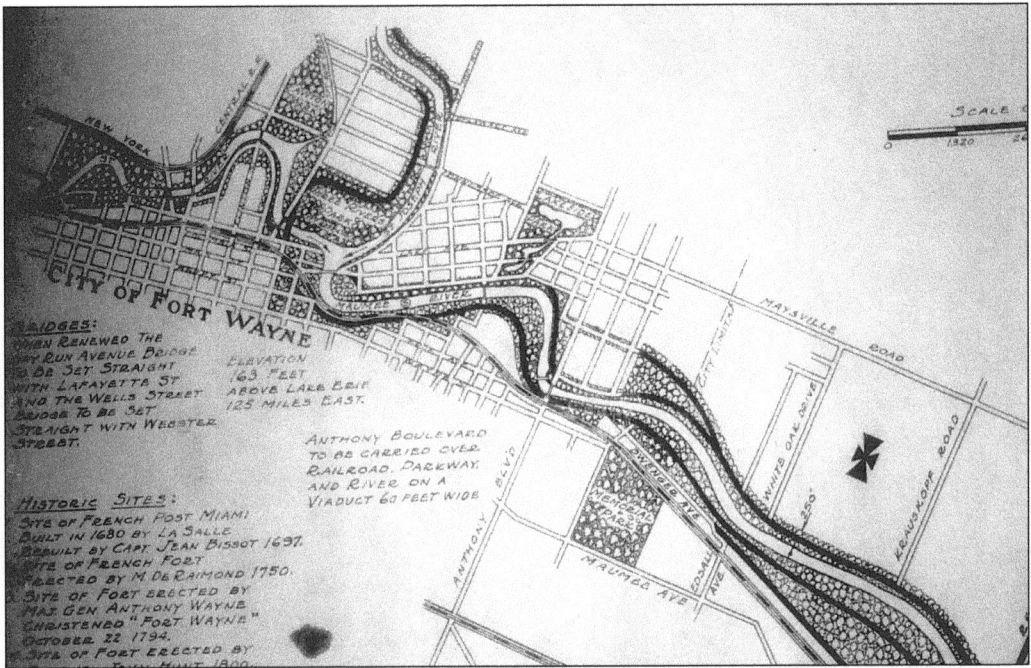

Another view of Hanna's extensive river-greenway plan shows development extending east from the thumb past Anthony Boulevard and Reed Road. (AC/FW Historical Society.)

In the 1930s, billboards began promoting the plan for Three Rivers Park. Central to the theme was development of the thumb into a park and festival center. This photograph shows plans for additional sports facilities in what is now Headwaters Park.

In 1930, downtown Fort Wayne was growing with the recent completion of the tallest building in Indiana, the Lincoln Tower, shown in this picture. In the upper portion is the thumb that now houses a National Guard Armory as well as other buildings. (AC Public Library.)

During the devastating years of the Great Depression, what is now Phase I was a Shantytown, filled with tarpaper shacks just south of where the Jail Flats once stood. Hundreds of families lived in this area at its peak in 1933. The path in the far right is Calhoun Street. (AC/FW Historical Society.)

In this photo, League Stadium is visible near the center. To the immediate upper left is the new National Guard Armory building. In the far upper left—and just barely visible—is the first Fort Wayne National Bank, now Star Financial Bank. (AC/FW Historical Society.)

Pictured is one of the many shacks located in what is now Headwaters Park in the 1930s. (AC/FW Historical Society.)

These two photographs from the late 1930s show a more prosperous downtown and a growing skyline. The thumb is now devoid of Shantytowns and boasts more industrial development. (AC/FW Historical Society.)

The realities of flooding appear again in May of 1943, when many parts of the city are again under water. While this flood was not as bad as the 1913 flood, it caused wide spread damage, as in the south end of Lawton Park directly across the river from the thumb. Clinton Street Bridge is in the background.

Clinton Street next to the city power plant is closed due to high water. The power plant became Science Central in 1995.

Harrison Street Bridge crosses over the Saint Mary's River to the west of the thumb. The City Light sign is visible as it stands along Calhoun Street in what is now the west portion of Headwaters Park. (AC Public Library.)

A familiar building with access from both Clinton and Calhoun Streets was the National Guard Armory. The building was completed in 1930 and stood until late 1997. The Headwaters Park Commission had hoped to renovate the building for festival use and indoor winter activities. However, it was beyond repair when it was acquired in 1995 and was razed two years later to make way for the final phase of the park. (Ed Welling, Grinsfelder and Associates Architects.)

Aerial views of downtown Fort Wayne show the Harrison and Wells Street bridges in the late 1930s and the recently completed water filtration plant just to the east of the thumb at the junction of the three rivers. (AC/FW Historical Society.)

These two photographs show the before and after of one of the developments that allowed the north side of the city to grow rapidly in the late 1950s. The elevation of the Nickel Plate Railroad was completed over the tracks built eight decades earlier on the bed of the Wabash and Erie Canal. This structure, at the south end of what is now Headwaters Park, allowed motorists to travel undeterred by the dozens of trains that crossed the city each day. (AC/FW Historical Society.)

Development of the thumb evolved over the decades. By 1970, the 30 acres was dotted with business and commerce, as downtown real estate was rare and valuable. In the background is the nearly completed Fort Wayne National Bank Building, which opened later that year. (AC/FW Historical Society.)

Fort Wayne was the scene of another major flood in March of 1978. Clinton Street, the major artery entering the city from the north, was closed to traffic by high water for the first time at the northern portion of what is now Headwaters Park. Flood waters encroach upon the Spot Home Center and Poinsette Motors. In the background are the Lincoln Tower, City-County Building, and Fort Wayne National Bank. (AC/FW Historical Society.)

Another view of the Flood of 1978 shows parked vehicles on the Clinton Street Bridge with the water covering the street in the background. All north and south traffic had to be rerouted on Lafayette Street/Spy Run Avenue, which was previously one way northbound. Severe traffic problems resulted from this flood, as well as millions of dollars in damage. (AC/FW Historical Society.)

These two photographs show the dichotomy of the landscape from 1978 and 1996. The 1978 picture shows the Hector Garcia sculpture of Little Turtle surrounded by the emerging waters of the oncoming flood. Supposedly, the water reached the great Indian Chief's knees during the height of the 1982 flood. The 1996 picture (below) shows a dry landscape and the remarkable growth of the pine trees planted along the sculpture twenty years earlier. (Top photo courtesy of AC/FW Historical Society; bottom photo courtesy of Gabe Delobbe for Headwaters Park.)

The dichotomy of the land surrounding the replica of Historic Fort Wayne is visible from these two pictures. Sandbags were placed along the bank of the Saint Mary's River to protect businesses in the thumb in 1978. The Old Fort, surrounded by water, is slightly visible in the background. In this late 1970s photograph, the replica of the Old Fort is shown in drier times and guarded by a sentry. (AC/FW Historical Society.)

This aerial view shows most of the thumb under water, including Clinton Street, in March of 1982. This was the second highest flood on record, destroying millions of dollars worth of property and inventory. Valiant efforts at sandbagging to save homes and businesses earned Fort Wayne the title "The City That Saved Itself." (Ed Welling, Grinsfelder Associates Architects.)

Perhaps two of the most well-known pictures of the thumb are the two views taken by the *News Sentinel* (above) and the *Journal Gazette* (below) on March 15, 1982. (Top photograph courtesy of the *Fort Wayne News Sentinel*; bottom photograph courtesy of the *Fort Wayne Journal Gazette*.)

Flood waters inundated the thumb and low lying areas to the north. (*Fort Wayne Journal Gazette.*)

This picture of the area west of the thumb along Main Street exemplifies the broad devastation. (*Fort Wayne Journal Gazette.*)

When the waters receded in the early
spring of 1982, the city cleaned up and
repaired itself and then put together a
plan to protect itself from future floods.
Mayor Win Moses, Jr, along with city and
county leaders, decided to promote major
flood prevention efforts in the 1980s. A
plan to widen the Maumee River, build
flood protection walls, and clear the thumb
of buildings and development, would
become a major theme for the Summit
City over the next two decades. The top
photograph was taken in the late 1970s,
and the lower photograph in the late 1980s.
(Both photographs courtesy Ed Welling
of Grinsfelder Associates Architects.)

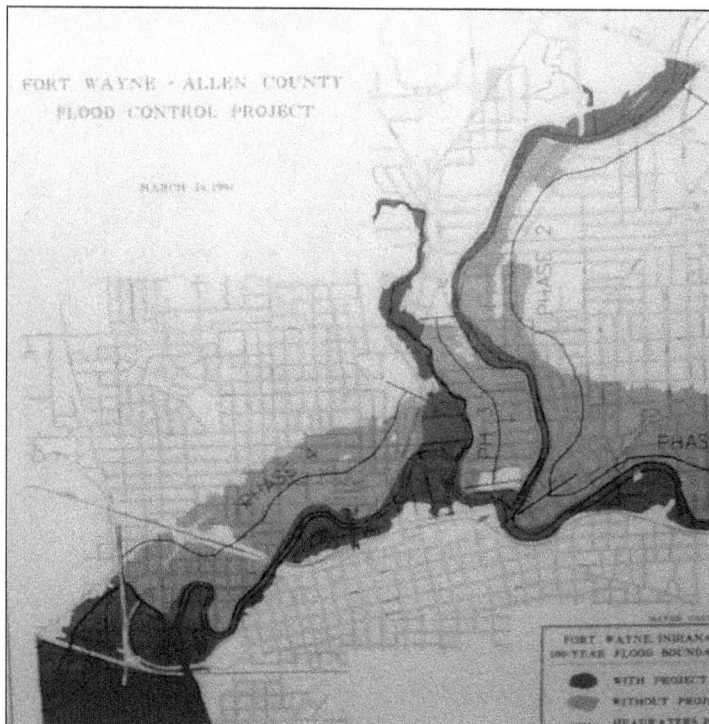

FORT WAYNE · ALLEN COUNTY
FLOOD CONTROL PROJECT

MARCH 14, 1994

PHASE 2

PHAS

PHAS

FORT WAYNE INDIANA
100-YEAR FLOOD BOUNDA

WITH PROJECT
WITHOUT PROJ
HEADWATERS 2

One of the last building developments at the southwest portion of the thumb was the new Allen County Jail, located just south of the old Jail Flats and the National Guard Armory, visible at the bottom of this picture taken in 1980. (AC Public Library.)

This map shows the vast area of the city affected by the half dozen or so major floods during the past nine decades. The three flood control initiatives, when completed, would prevent over 4,000 homes and businesses in this area from being damaged by high water. (Map courtesy of the City of Fort Wayne.)

Four

FLOOD CONTROL

Flood control efforts began to draw more interest after the 1913 flood, but serious efforts to address the problem did not take place until the early 1980s. Three major efforts were introduced and completed over the next two decades. The Maumee River Widening project, somewhat controversial to environmentalists, hastened the flow of water on the east side of the city. New and higher flood protection walls were constructed by the Army Corps of Engineers. They protected another 4,400 homes and businesses from being damaged by water. And, finally, Headwaters Park was constructed to manage flood control in the "thumb," and promote recreation and economic activity in the downtown area.

As early as 1871, a cartographer named Lowry included the thumb on a map and realized it could play a substantial role in flood mitigation. The effort to build a park around the rivers was first proposed in 1912 as part of a flood control and downtown revitalization project. Nationally-known landscape architect George Kessler presented a detailed plan to the city just prior to the 1913 flood. The plan was permanently delayed by the advent of World War I. Another plan was presented by consultant Robert Hanna in 1929. It was more extensive than the Kessler plan and extended further along the rivers. It was not until the early 1980s that Fort Wayne architect Eric R. Kuhne, a former city planner under Mayor Ivan Lebamoff, was commissioned to design a flood control plan in the thumb that would provide for a park and a premier festival center. It would also serve as a model for flood control in other sections of the country.

The Headwaters State Park Alliance was formed in 1984 to facilitate Kuhne's plan into a sweeping state park, boasting, among other things, a huge spray fountain at the confluence of the three rivers. When the state decided not to participate in building another state park in northeast Indiana, the State Park Alliance folded in 1986. The Headwaters Park Commission was formed in 1987 to oversee development of a city park, rather than a state park. It was to become the operating body and exercise essential "public functions" as the legislative and governing body of the project. This power was granted under state law, but the Commission became the only such body of its kind in the entire state.

Mayor Win Moses, Jr. appointed the first board members before leaving office. Mayor Paul Helmke appointed several others. The remainder were appointed by Allen County Commissioners or other entities. The Headwaters Park Commission was a governmental entity made possible by an interlocal agreement and sanctioned by state statue. The agreement gave the Commission eminent domain powers and control over the design and implementation of Kuhne's plan, as implemented by local architects Alan Grinsfelder and Ed Welling of Grinsfelder Associates, and landscape architects Kevin McCrory and Greg Byrd of the LandPlan Group. The commission was also the arm to raise private dollars to build the new park, as most government funds could only be used for land acquisition, business relocation, building demolition, and environmental remediation. The Fort Wayne Redevelopment Commission, led by Ron Fletcher and Loren

Kravig, became a partner in purchasing land and preparing the site for construction. They appropriated over $5 million through the Light-Lease Fund, authored by Mayor Ivan Lebamoff, for this purpose. The Headwaters Park Commission was made up of thirteen citizen members and began meeting in 1988. In addition to overseeing and implementing development plans, the Commission raised nearly $10 million for construction and an endowment. Local architect and park enthusiast John Shoaff was elected president and served for the thirteen years of the Commission's life, ending in March 2001.

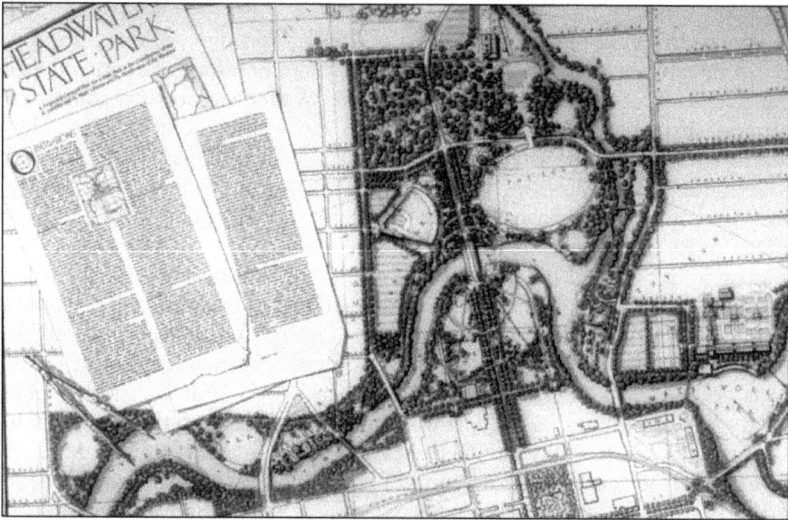

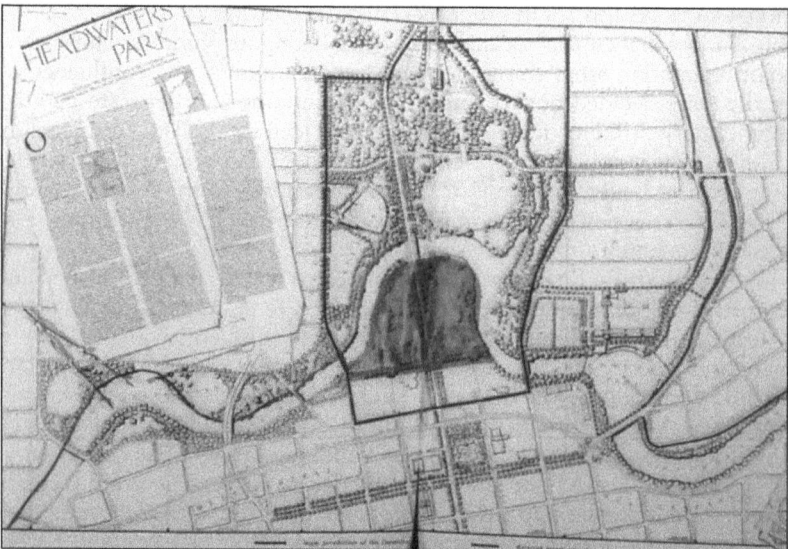

After the Flood of 1982, architect and former city planner Eric R. Kuhne was commissioned by the city to draw up a plan to clear the thumb of buildings and obstacles to the flood waters and create a downtown park and festival center. Kuhne took inspiration from the earlier plans submitted by Kessler and Hanna and presented the Headwaters State Park plan in January of 1985. As seen in the two sketches, the plans presented earlier in the century evolved into a more dynamic setting, but with much of the earlier designs intact. (Plans courtesy of Headwaters Park Alliance.)

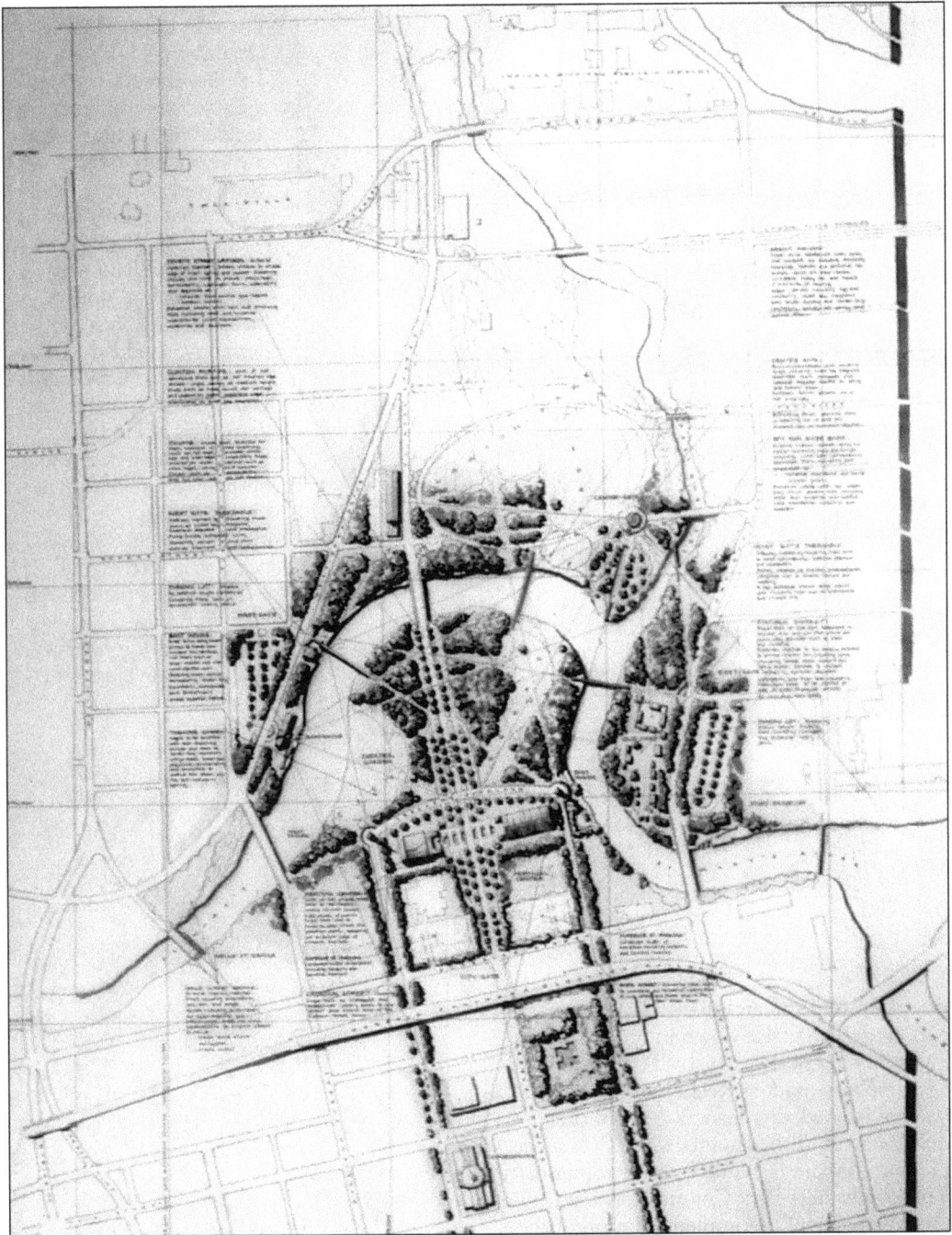

The State of Indiana had earlier expressed interest in funding this portion of Fort Wayne's flood control initiative, hence the name of Headwaters State Park. Kuhne penned the name for a sweeping park to be built where the Saint Mary's and Saint Joseph Rivers form the headwaters of the Maumee River. His design emphasized many aspects of Hanna's Three Rivers Park. However, when the state government withdrew support for a state park at the confluence, Kuhne had to redesign his plan and slightly change the name. (Architectural plan of Eric R. Kuhne, property of the Headwaters Park Alliance.)

HEADWATERS PARK

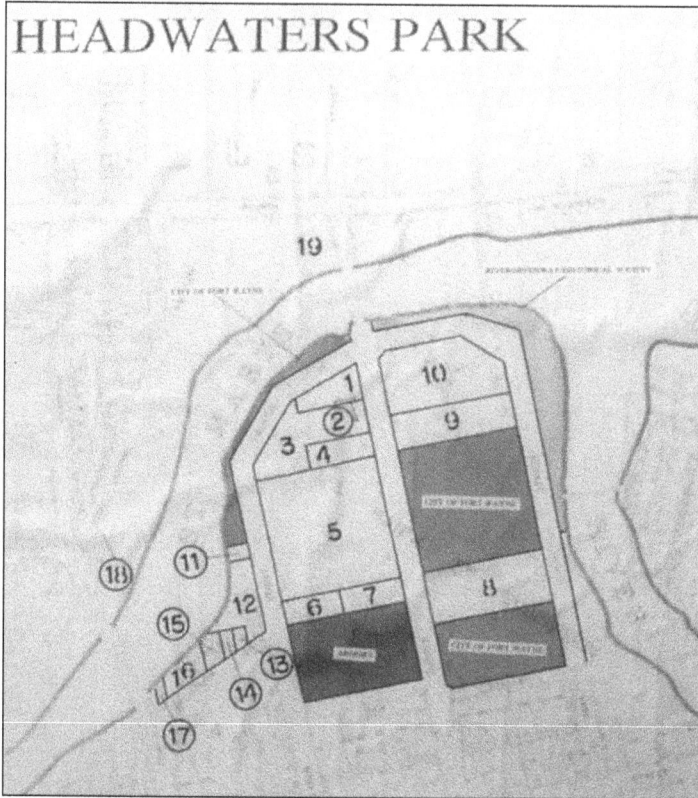

19

The construction of Headwaters Park took a different direction when the state government decided not to fund the entire project. State leaders, however, committed to help the City of Fort Wayne purchase the land with "Build Indiana" dollars. Nearly 2 million state dollars were added to over $5 million in "City Light Lease" funds to purchase 23 parcels of land in the thumb. Over a dozen small businesses, the National Guard Armory, and other city departments would be relocated to higher ground so the park could be built on the 30 acres of the thumb. (City of Fort Wayne Redevelopment Department.)

Eric Kuhne's 1985 architectural plan for the park had to be scaled down in order to meet budgetary restrictions. Instead of a grand 170 acre state park as Kessler and Hanna had envisioned, city leaders decided that development of the thumb, which was most prone to flooding, should become top priority. The Headwaters Park Commission was formed to take charge of the implementation of the park and to raise over half of the projected budget through private dollars. Design of the western portion of the thumb was proposed first. This became Phase I, about ten acres highlighted by trees, flower gardens, and open green space. (Architectural plan of Eric R. Kuhne property of Headwaters Park Alliance.)

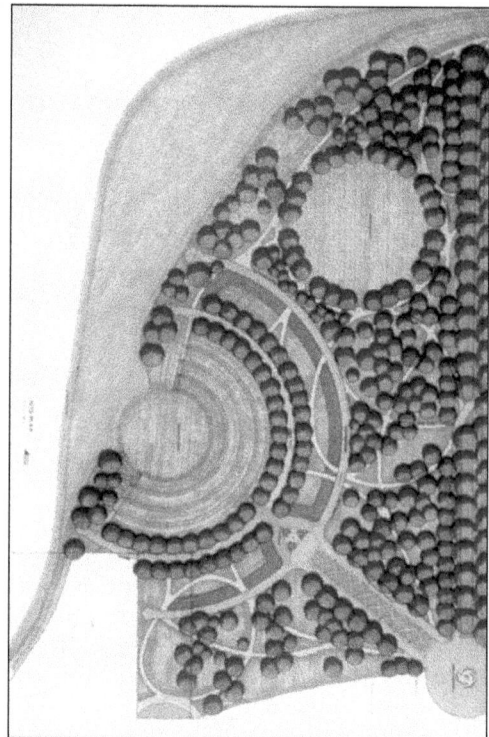

In the early 1990s, the city and the new Headwaters Park Commission agreed to the plan to develop Headwaters Park with Kuhne's design. The project was divided into four phases of development so there would be ample time to fine tune the design and raise the nearly 10 million in private dollars needed. Here, Phase II basically became the other half of the thumb with more open green space, trees, and flower gardens. In addition, a major source fountain would attract more people to this side of the park, which is about twelve acres. (Kuhne plan, Headwaters Park Alliance.)

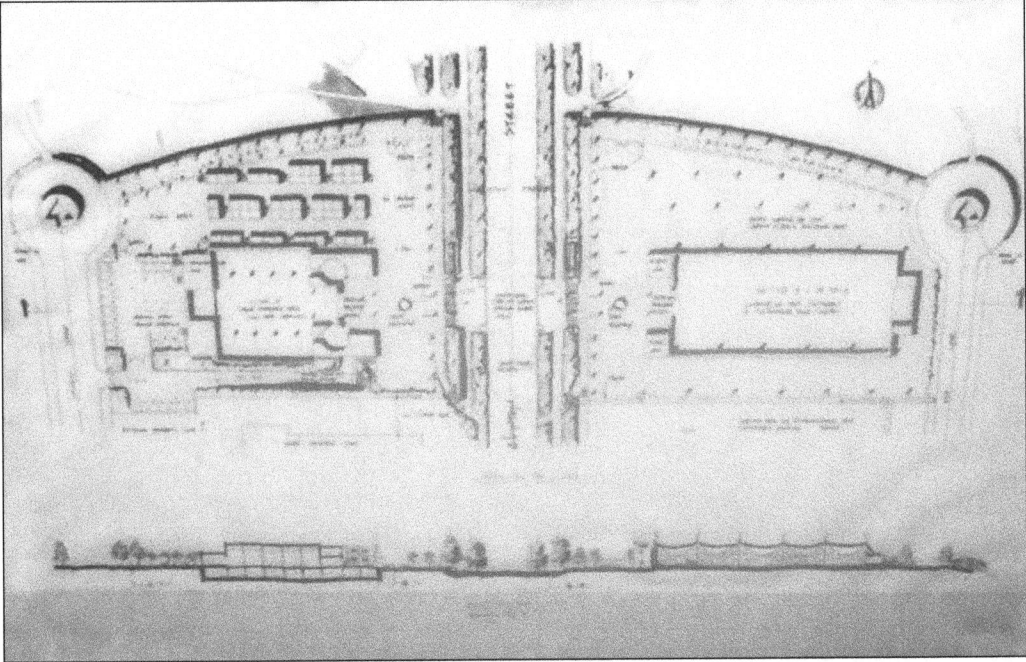

A large festival center built on high ground and just to the south of the low lying thumb area became Phases III and IV of the project. Kuhne's design called for the eight to ten acre area to become a permanent site for major festivals and summer activities. The state-of-the-art festival center would be able to hold thousands of people gathered under tents and a pavilion. (Kuhne Plan, Headwaters Park Alliance.)

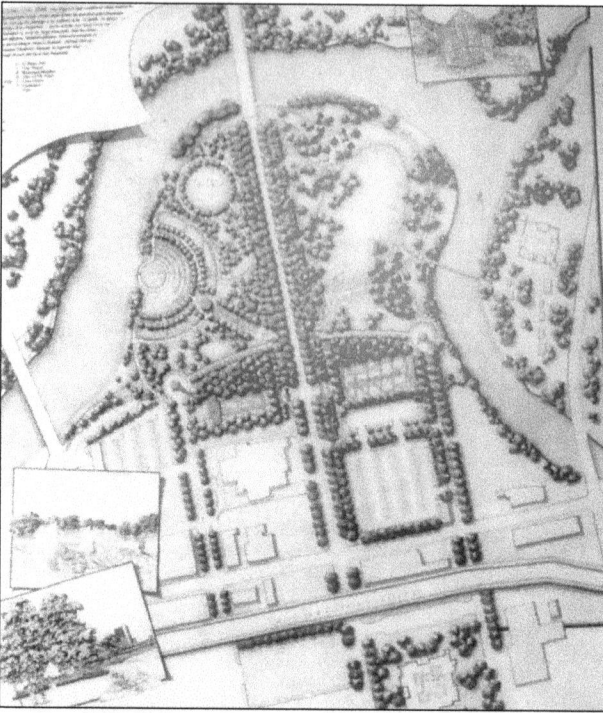

The Headwaters Park Commission played a major role in working with Kuhne and architects Tom Navin, Alan Grinsfelder, Ed Welling, and Kevin McCrory in seeing the plan grow and evolve into a development that would be beautiful and functional, as well as provide flood mitigation for the city. The hope was for Headwaters Park to become the central gathering place for festivals, not-for-profit events, weddings, receptions, family gatherings, and picnics. (Kuhne Plan, Headwaters Park Alliance.)

A model of what was proposed for the final product in 1994. Early plans called for renovation of the National Guard Armory Building, as well as construction of a large reflecting pond and pedestrian bridges crossing the Saint Mary's River. The plan was scaled back to meet budgetary considerations, but most of Kuhne's major themes remained intact over the next several years of fund raising, design changes, and construction. (Eric R. Kuhne and Associates and Grinsfelder Associates Architects.)

Five

PARK CONSTRUCTION

The territory under the purview of the Headwaters Park Commission was nearly 200 acres bounded by Superior Street to the south, Spy Run Avenue to the east, Elizabeth Street to the north, and Harrison Street to the west. The grand master plan included all of this area in its recommendations for urban improvements and flood control downtown. There was a great deal of interest to rehabilitate this entire space in the mid 1980s, but the funding did not exist to take on such a large project. Hence, the Commission was primarily concerned with clearing the "thumb" of all structures for flood mitigation. Once that goal was achieved, a secondary goal was the development of a major urban landscaped park. The new green grassy land will serve as a sponge and absorb flood waters providing nearly 22 acres for containment. When dry, the park serves as a scenic and recreational use area near the confluence of the three rivers; a linkage between downtown and the Rivergreenway trail system; and a venue for festivals, weddings, receptions, and charitable events. To that end, Headwaters Park has become a hub in downtown Fort Wayne: a major gathering place each summer, providing a new and permanent home for the city's many festivals.

In 1993, the Commission set out to rehabilitate the 30 acre thumb in four phases of development. Construction on the west portion, or Phase I, was begun in the spring of 1994 and dedicated on September 10, 1995. Construction of the other three phases would be completed as funding became available. Phase II (essentially the eastern portion of the thumb) was developed and dedicated on September 14, 1996. The festival plaza was built and dedicated as Phase III, the eastern portion, on June 7, 1997. Phase IV, the western portion, was completed in late 1999. It was dedicated, along with the entire completed project, on October 22, 1999. The project was brought in within the time frame originally laid out and within budget. A surplus of private dollars raised was invested as a partial maintenance endowment for operating the park and festival center. Headwaters Park was turned over to the City of Fort Wayne, as originally proposed, on January 1, 2000. The cost of the entire project, including construction, land acquisition, environmental remediation, salaries, fees, and a maintenance endowment of $850,000, was just under $16.9 million.

In 2000, the Commission offered to continue its work and develop much of the remaining 170 acres within its jurisdiction by continuing its public private partnership with government. However, agreement on moving forward with the city and county could not be reached, and the Commission met its expiration date on March 18, 2001.

In a major departure from park management, the Headwaters Park Alliance, Inc. was formed in 2000 to become the managing agent of the 30 acres in the thumb. While the property belongs to the city, the park and festival center is managed by a private not-for-profit corporation dedicated to the full time management and quality maintenance of the city's new central park. The Alliance has raised private dollars for this purpose and manages the maintenance endowment that is also providing an income stream. This arrangement saves the taxpayers money and relieves the Fort Wayne Department of Parks and Recreation from the responsibility of maintaining the park. The Alliance has pledged to raise additional dollars for the maintenance endowment and make additional capital improvements in the park, with approval and participation of the city. In 2002, the Alliance began its second full year of operation under the leadership of Eleanor H. Marine, president, a former member of the Headwaters Park Commission. There are thirteen other board members.

Today, over 30 groups of individuals reserve the festival center nearly every weekend from April through October for festivals, not-for-profit events, weddings, receptions, and children's activities. It is estimated that over 600,000 people attend events each year, more than two-thirds of them during the Three Rivers Festival in July. As Fort Wayne approaches its 208th birthday, it has become clear that Headwaters Park is truly the city's central gathering place and premier center for recreation.

(Unless otherwise noted, all of the following pictures are the sole property and courtesy of the Headwaters Park Alliance, Inc.; Geoff Paddock, Executive Director.)

The challenge that lay ahead was to acquire all the properties in the thumb, relocate the businesses to higher ground, and remove the buildings and concrete to make way for a park. The above photograph and the three opposite ones show a few of the properties acquired and demolished in the fall of 1993. (Ed Welling, Grinsfelder Associates Architects.)

67

These two photographs show the first building taken down by the demolition equipment at a ceremony on October 26, 1993. The Remington Rand Building on Clinton Street met its demise first, followed by Hubcap Express, Three Rivers Archery, Jan's Furniture, and Auto Diagnosis. A billboard and a paved parking lot are also removed to make way for construction of Phase I of Headwaters Park.

Top: A former service station, at the corner of Clinton and Calhoun Streets, awaits demolition in the fall of 1993.

Bottom Left: On October 22, 1994, the city's 200th birthday, people gather on the Phase I construction site. Ian Rolland, retired chief executive officer of Lincoln National Corporation and fundraising chair of the Headwaters project, speaks at the microphone.

Bottom Right: The bicentennial time capsule's commemorative plaque, located in Phase I, indicates it will be unearthed on October 22, 2094, the city's 300th birthday.

Construction of Phase I progresses in the spring of 1995, as Martin demolition trucks haul thousands of tons of debris away from the site just north of the National Guard Armory Building.

Phase I construction is seen from the National City Bank Building. The smoke stack of the Armory protrudes just beyond the Allen County Jail. To the north of the park stands Science Central and its three smoke stacks.

Construction in the summer of 1995 results in the many miles of sidewalks that grace the 30 acres of park and festival center. Pictured in the upper right of this picture is the bicentennial time capsule, buried near the Clinton Street sidewalk and dedicated on October 22, 1994. Another angle shows the first of the Hyde Park-style park benches installed near a lamppost.

From the south overlook, a view of mulch being added to the Phase I site. Two overlooks allow visitors to gaze across the Saint Mary's River. This side of the park also contains more than 200 trees in dozens of varieties. The Bridge Meadow is so named because it could eventually serve as the starting point for a pedestrian bridge built to accommodate wheelchairs across the Saint Mary's River. Crimson King Maple trees highlight this area of the park.

The following three photographs depict construction stages of the small stainless steel pavilion, known as the "fog dish," or the Foliatum. The idea behind the structure was to provide an ornamental object that would emit a mist and become an attraction to visitors. Concrete benches are added to provide a place to sit and enjoy the surroundings.

Workers in the summer of 1995 make final plantings for the dedication of Phase I. Headwaters Park contains numerous plants and vegetation designed to provide color and intrigue throughout the four seasons.

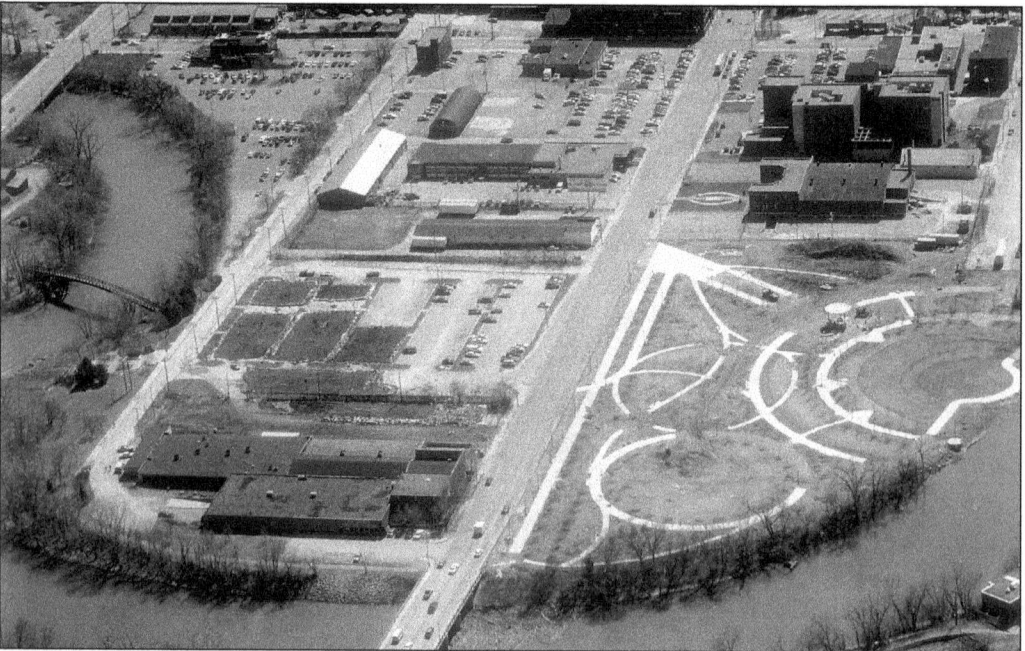

An aerial view shows a partially completed Phase I in the early spring of 1995. Some demolition on the east side of Clinton Street has begun, but many more properties must be acquired before this side of the street, Phase II, is ready for construction.

76

Dedication of Phase I occurs as people gather under the fog dish on September 10, 1995. Straw still covers freshly laid sod that will form much of the green area to absorb future flood waters. The dedication brings out special guests such as U.S. Congressman Mark Souder, right, seen here with Stephen and Kathleen Paddock.

The trees and plants in Phase I begin to show late summer color.

Opposite: Architect Eric Kuhne's vision of the Foliatum is seen here in a view of the model depicting its grandeur. Fog emanates from the top of the dish and around many of the surrounding flower gardens. The photograph within the poster shows the magnitude of the mist on a cool evening.

HEADWATERS PARK

Dense fog gathers in the park. It is regulated so the mist dissipates before it becomes a security risk.

The fog surrounding the flower gardens provides a beautiful backdrop for a wedding ceremony in Phase I. The first wedding in the park occurred on September 1, 1996 celebrating the union of Karen Bobilier and John Gerni, a member of the Headwaters Park Commission. The park hosts several weddings each season.

Construction begins on the east side of Clinton Street, or Phase II, in the summer of 1996. Architect Thomas Navin, far right, inspects the flood protection wall.

The large source fountain that has become so popular with children fills with water. The Fontanelle has three large jets of water that shoot up and down at a height of six to ten feet in the air.

Another aerial view of the construction site is visible in the summer of 1995. The west side of Phase I is covered with straw to protect it from the hot sun. Several buildings on the east side must be acquired before this portion of the park can be completed.

The Phase II side also has rows of sidewalks where triangular indentations have been made to provide wheelchair access into the meadows and gathering places. Seen here is the large meadow. Several hundred trees, as well as strategically placed fog misters, also grace this side of the park.

The dedication of the second phase of development takes place on September 14, 1996. The ceremony is highlighted with the inauguration of the source fountain, or Fontanelle.

Dedication speakers include, from left to right, John Shoaff, president of the Headwaters Park Commission, design architect Eric Kuhne, Indiana's First Lady Judy O'Bannon, and Mayor Paul Helmke.

Construction of Phase III, the eastern portion of the festival center, begins along with the opening of Phase II in 1996. This photograph shows the foundation for the festival buildings and large concrete plaza soon to become the home of dozens of festivals and other events that bring in over 500,000 people to Headwaters Park each year.

Construction of the east festival plaza continues in the winter of 1997. The northern block building houses rest rooms, while the southern is an office and storage room for festivals.

More work is done on the concrete plaza that also hosts a fountain flush with the ground.

These two pictures show construction on the Water Field, the name for the festival plaza fountain. This water feature has 44 jets that shoot water as high as fifteen feet in the air. It is operated on timers, and children often scream with anticipation as they wait for the water to bubble up after retreating to the base. The water is recycled, and chlorine is added for sanitary protection.

A key component of Headwaters Park is flood protection. Here, part of the raised flood protection wall surrounding the Barr Street turn around is visible during construction of Phase III in the spring of 1997.

The above picture along with the images on the next two pages show dedication day of the third phase of development and the east festival plaza on June 7, 1997. The Headwaters Park name is proudly emblazoned on the flood protection wall near the entrance to the plaza.

A large cast iron triangle denotes the row of Autumn Purple Ash trees sponsored by the Downtown Rotary Club.

The park's second fountain rears up between the tent posts on the festival plaza.

The dedication of the East Festival Plaza is highlighted by the inauguration of the plaza fountain, or Water Field, as named by the architects.

The event coincides with the first festival hosted by this new state of the art plaza on June 7, 1997: the Fort Wayne Black Expo. Since that day, over a dozen festivals and many smaller events have called this plaza their home over the past five years.

In July 1997, the Three Rivers Festival was held as progress on the thumb continued. The double wide tents are visible on the festival plaza, with other tents and vendors set up in the parched Great Meadow of Phase II. The National Guard Armory, visible in the lower left of the picture,

is being prepped for demolition. (Aerial photo property of the Headwaters Park Alliance, Inc.; photo provided by John Escosa of Stedman Studios of Fort Wayne.)

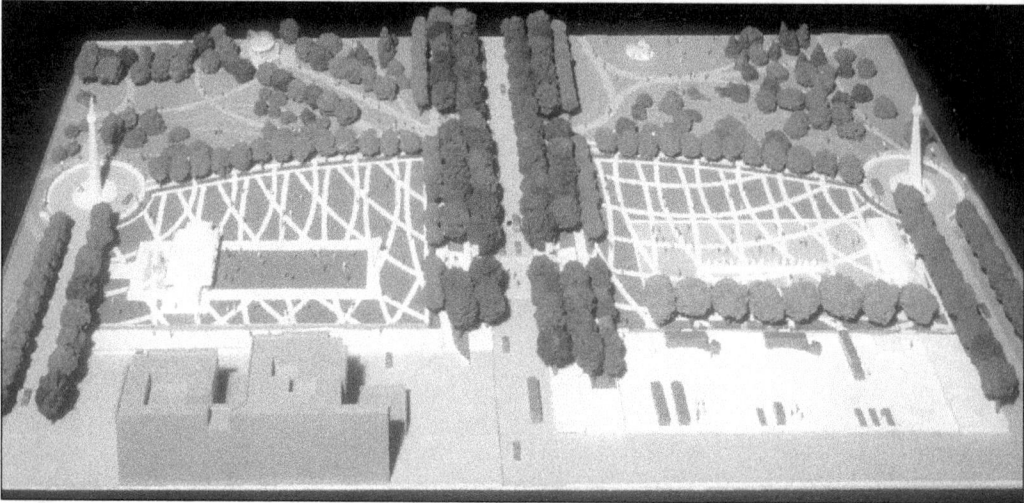

Architects Eric R. Kuhne and Associates and Grinsfelder Associates present the model of the completed plaza in late 1997 as the project enters its final stage.

In the spring of 1999, the construction of the west plaza and open-air pavilion take shape in what would soon be Phase IV.

The final phase concludes in the fall of 1999, and a formal dedication of the entire project is held on October 22, 1999, Fort Wayne's 205th birthday.

Bagpiper Justin Zolnik performs on the new west festival plaza.

Design architect Eric Kuhne speaks eloquently of his dream to reclaim the thumb, and hundreds of people gather under the new pavilion to watch the ceremony. At left is Governor Frank O'Bannon.

The ribbon cutting of The Headwaters Flood Control and Park Project officially opens the new park to the public on October 22, 1999. Participants include Headwaters Park Commissioners Judy Zehner and Gary Wasson; John Shoaff, President; State Representative Ben GiaQuinta; Geoff Paddock, Executive Director; and Indiana Governor Frank O'Bannon. A special tribute is made at the park dedication to board member Janet Olofsen McCaulay, who had passed away in August.

John Escosa of Stedman Studios in Fort Wayne took this final aerial photograph on October 15, 1999. Finally, after seven years of hard work and nearly eight decades of dreaming, the thumb has been reshaped into a beautiful central park and activity center for hundreds of thousands of people each year. Both Fort Wayne newspapers and the television media proclaim Headwaters Park one of the most significant accomplishments to occur in the city over the past fifty years. (Drawing courtesy of *Fort Wayne News Sentinel*, June 23, 1999.)

Two plaques mark the many contributors and volunteers who worked tirelessly to see the project to fruition. The dedication plaque (right) lists the thirteen current Headwaters Park Commissioners, as well as former commissioners, architects, and consultants. Of particular note was the excellent work of general contractors Brooks Construction Company and Hamilton Hunter Builders, both of Fort Wayne, who supplied local labor. The other plaque (below) denotes the 100 top financial donors who contributed $5,000 or more to the project.

HEADWATERS FLOOD CONTROL AND PARK PROJECT

Dedicated October 22, 1999

Paul Helmke, Mayor

HEADWATERS PARK COMMISSION	FORMER COMMISSIONERS
John H. Shoaff, President	C. Philip Andorfer
Melvyn Griswold	Timothy S. Borne
Judith Zehner	Janie Davis
Eleanor H. Marine	Archie Lunsey
Molly McCray	Mark GiaQuinta
Janet McCaulay	Richard Groves
John P. Gerni	Ternae Jordan
John D. Walda	Daniel K. Leininger
John Stafford	Michael Marchese, Jr.
Gary Wasson	Dwight Mosley
Linda K. Bloom	Rebecca Ravine
Martin A. Bender	Charles Redd
C. James Owen	Carl D. Rolfsen
Ian Rolland, Fund Raising Chairman	Joe Ruffolo
Geoff Paddock, Executive Director	Cheryl Taylor
	Charles J. Weinraub
	Jack R. Worthman

ARCHITECTS AND CONSULTANTS

Eric R. Kuhne & Associates
Grinsfelder Associates Architects
McCrory Associates Landscape Architects
Matson Consulting Engineers
Lougheed and Associates

GENERAL CONTRACTORS

Brooks Construction Company
Hamilton Hunter Builders

HEADWATERS PARK MAJOR CONTRIBUTORS

City of Fort Wayne	Ernst & Young LLP
State of Indiana	Richard and Mary Louise Doermer
Foellinger Foundation	Insurance & Risk Management
Lincoln National Foundation	PriceWaterhouseCoopers
English, Bonter, Mitchell Foundation	Rod and Marcia Howard
Edward M. Wilson Family Foundation	Glenbrook Square Management
McMillen Foundation	Merrill Lynch
Fort Wayne Bicentennial Celebration Council	Eleanor and Lockwood Marine
Journal Gazette Foundation	O'Daniel Oldsmobile
GTE Telephone Operations	Barrett & McNagny
Morrill Charitable Foundation	Brooks Construction
Northern Indiana Public Service Company	C & E Schust Foundation
Fort Wayne National Bank	Central Soya Company
Fort Wayne Community Foundation	Ellison Bakery
American Electric Power	Haller & Colvin
Kuhne Foundation	Irmscher Suppliers
Franklin Electric Company	Flora Dale Krouse Foundation
Kelley Foundation	Martin, Inc.
Norwest Bank Indiana	Poinsatte-Altman Foundation
Zollner Foundation	Sfedd Foundation
Bank One	Florence & Paul Staehle Foundation
Sarah Niezer Hall Estate	John H. Shoaff and Julie Donnell
Byron H. Somers Foundation	Wilda Gene Marcus
Cole Foundation	Rea Magnet Wire Company
Dana Corporation	Goldstine Knapke Company
Do It Best	Peg Perego USA
Fort Wayne Park Foundation	Acordia/O'Rourke
ITT Aerospace/Communications	Anthony Wayne Corporation
Phelps Dodge Magnet Wire	Azar, Inc.
Physicians Health Plan	Brotherhood Mutual Insurance
Raytheon Systems Company	Colwell/General
Shoaff Family	June E. Enoch
Tokheim Corporation	Federated Media of Fort Wayne
Magee-O'Connor Foundation	Fisher Brothers Paper
Superior Essex	Glenbrook Dodge-Hyundai
Barnes & Thornburg	Hillard Lyons
Psi Iota Xi - Pi Chapter	Michael & Robin Holley
ME Raker Foundation	Home Loan Bank
News-Sentinel	Diane S. Humphrey
Waterfield Foundation	ICON
Fort Wayne Rotary Club	Mr. and Mrs. Joseph F. Jones
Baker & Daniels	Kevin and Pamela Kelly
Robert I. Goldstine	Jane L. and Donald R. Keltsch
Knight Foundation	Kroger Company
Mattel Power Wheels	Jackson and Carol Lehman
North American Van Lines	Michael and Grace Mastrangelo
Ian and Mimi Rolland	Geoff Paddock
AALCO Distributing Company	Pizza Hut of Fort Wayne
Almet, Inc.	Donald Sherman
Don R. Fruchey, Inc.	Williams College
Meijer, Inc.	Don and Virginia Wolf

While the project is formally dedicated on October 22, 1999, a few other pieces are added within the next year. On October 22, 2000, the Hamilton Sculpture denoting the significant contribution of Agnes, Alice, and Edith Hamilton to the development of our city is dedicated. Many generous donors offered the series of sculptures as a birthday gift to the city. Patty Martone, a renowned educator and civic volunteer, headed the project.

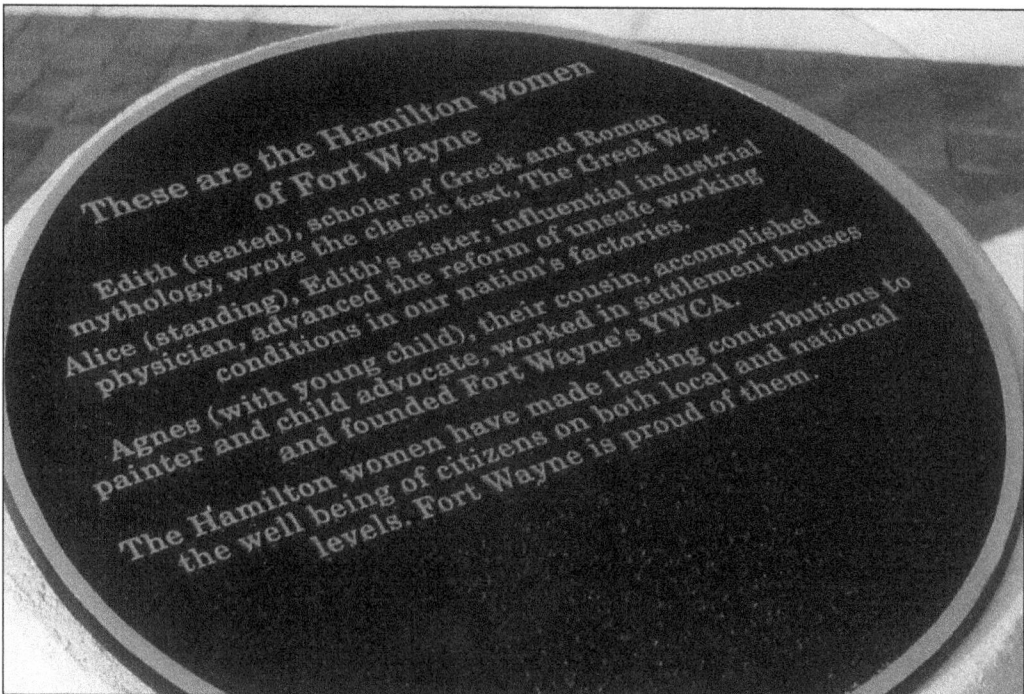

These are the Hamilton women of Fort Wayne

Edith (seated), scholar of Greek and Roman mythology, wrote the classic text, The Greek Way. Alice (standing), Edith's sister, influential industrial physician, advanced the reform of unsafe working conditions in our nation's factories. Agnes (with young child), their cousin, accomplished painter and child advocate, worked in settlement houses and founded Fort Wayne's YWCA. The Hamilton women have made lasting contributions to the well being of citizens on both local and national levels. Fort Wayne is proud of them.

That same year, other plaques denoting special gifts and historical significance are added. Of special importance are thirteen triangular cast iron plaques (three of them shown here) that tell the history of the thumb and surrounding area. Today, one can walk the east Great Meadow in a counter clockwise direction and read about the historical development of the Headwaters area, from the melting of the glaciers 10,000 years ago to the 1999 dedication.

Ornamental lamp posts and benches line the east flood protection wall, known as the Crescent Overlook. The majestic Foliatum stands among the autumn trees and native Indiana grasses.

One of the many daily park visitors relaxes while sitting on a Hyde Park bench.

Pictured is one of the dedication plaques displayed by the Donor Gates at the entrance to the east festival plaza. Attractive ornamental gates that surround the plaza provide security during the many events of the season.

A serene view of the Saint Mary's River is visible through the North Overlook on the west side of Phase I. The natural habitats of native foul and animals were left intact so their lifestyle would not be interrupted. Park patrons can still see beavers building dams, ducks nesting on the riverbank, and birds living in the nearly 600 trees growing in all four sections of the thumb.

106

Dozens of flower gardens, designed by landscape architects of the LandPlan Group (formerly McCrory Associates), are dotted through out the park. The location of many of the gardens also provides a view of the city in the background. Nearly 2,200 engraved bricks are positioned on the Crescent Overlook walkways on both the eastern and western portion of the park. Thousands of plain triangular bricks are in place and available for future engravement.

An evening scene shows Chief Little Turtle standing watch over the land he loved and helped to settle two centuries earlier. Little Turtle was placed looking in the direction of the confluence of the three rivers, which he once described as the "glorious gateway" to the west.

Headwaters Park proves itself as a flood control project even before its completion. These three photographs from April 1997, show water filling the terrace garden amphitheater on the west side of Phase I and along the riverbank on the east side of Phase II. The thumb is designed to provide flood relief, as it will absorb spillage from the Saint Mary's River in its 20 acres of grass and meadows.

When dry, Headwaters Park creates the perfect venue for family events. The downtown skyline is visible behind a festival tent, as evening falls on a summer scene from 1999. The first regularly scheduled event of the year is the Easter Egg Hunt, sponsored by the Wayne Township Trustee's office.

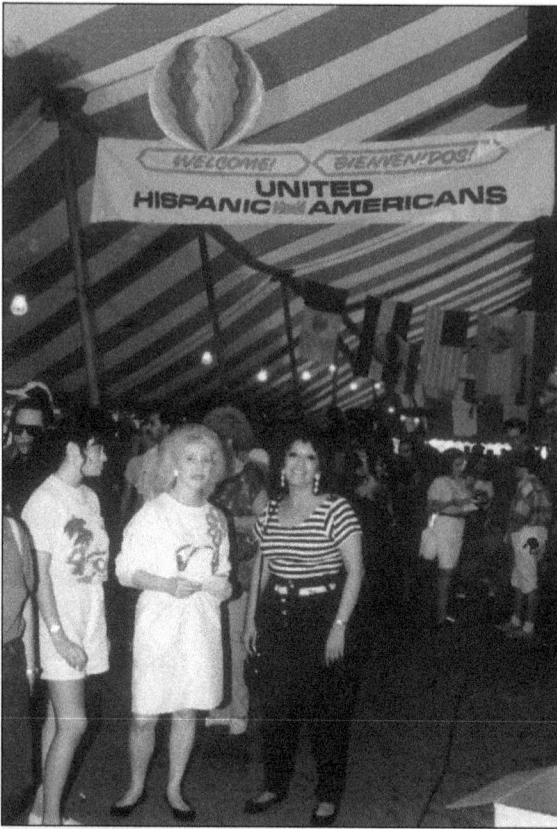

Even before the park was completed, many of the city's ethnic and family festivals called Headwaters Park their home. Here, La Gran Fiesta, or the Hispanicfest sponsored by United Hispanic Americans, holds their annual event on the east festival plaza in the late 1990s. (Photographs courtesy of United Hispanic Americans of Fort Wayne.)

A brass quintet from the Fort Wayne Philharmonic Orchestra performs in the shadow of the Foliatum during the dedication of Phase I on September 10, 1995. Similar musical groups have performed many times over the years, particularly in this area. The photo below shows an activity taking place in the terrace garden near the riverbank. The event marked Cancer Survivor Day in Headwaters Park on June 2, 1997.

One of many not-for-profit events that calls Headwaters Park home is the annual March of Dimes Walk-a-Thon. Participants gather under the pavilion on the west side on April 28, 2001.

By June of 2001, the annual Germanfest is the second largest festival held in the park and festival center. Over 60,000 people enjoy the four-day, mid-June, ethnic heritage celebration each year.

The Greekfest follows Germanfest in late June each year. The festival has grown each year it has made Headwaters Park its home. In June of 2001, the large festival tent and vendors set up in the south parking lot.

Another growing event is the annual Ribfest, shown here in 2001; it is now a four-day festival rivaling Germanfest as Headwaters Park's second largest event of the year. Rib vendors from around the country converge on the park in late June to prepare slabs of beef and pork to feed hungry people.

One of the largest fall events in Headwaters Park is the annual Rockin' Docs Music Festival, held in September. Doctors and other medical personnel perform in various rock 'n roll groups to raise funds for the Parkview Cancer Center Research Library at Parkview Memorial Hospital in Fort Wayne. This photograph was taken on September 14, 2001, under the pavilion.

The Fraternal Order of Police sponsors a Bicycle Helmet Day under the pavilion each spring and fall. Young cyclists are taught how to wear protective headgear and watch for oncoming traffic as they ride their bikes. Fort Wayne police officers Phil Geller and Art Norton are shown here in August of 2001.

The largest festival in Headwaters Park and the second largest in the State of Indiana is the Three Rivers Festival each July. Numerous activities bring almost a half a million people to the park and festival center over a ten-day period. North of the festival tents are interactive activities for children and adults. No TRF would be complete without food and beverages offered along the Barr Street Food Alley and in the park, near the fountain. The climactic event is the shooting of the fireworks from atop the National City Bank building on Sunday evening. The best view, of course, is from Headwaters Park.

By far, the most delightful place on a hot summer day or evening is in the fountain at Headwaters Park. Children and adults play in the interactive water feature just north of the flood protection on the east side. Three jets of water shoot as high as ten to twelve feet in the air. The water is chlorinated and recycled. Filters are cleaned on an hourly basis. Most participants love to play in the water, but some, like Carl Offerle (pg. 123), are content to stand in the middle and allow the walls of water to surround them.

Many dignitaries have visited Headwaters Park over the years including former Vice President Dan Quayle, Governor Frank O'Bannon, Lieutenant Governor Joe Kernan, and Congresswoman Jill Long Thompson. Here, United States Senator Richard G. Lugar of Indiana pauses with Kathleen Paddock, left, and Geoff Paddock, Executive Director, on July 10, 1999. Lugar was enjoying a tour of the 30-acre park and had just completed his duties as Grand Marshall of the Three Rivers Festival Parade.

American
Society of
Landscape
Architects

Honor
Award

presented by the

Indiana
Chapter

Headwaters Park
Fort Wayne, Indiana

The LandPlan Group, LLC

in recognition
of outstanding
professional
achievement

Headwaters Park Commission

The popularity of Headwaters Park has grown over the years. The park was awarded the Outstanding Achievement Award for concrete construction in 1996, the Outstanding Park Development Award by the Indiana Park and Recreation Association in 1997, the City Livability Award by the U.S. Conference of Mayors (one of five in the United States) in 1999, and the Honor Award (shown here) by the American Society of Landscape Architects in 2000. Events Coordinator Mike Holley, Leeper's Lawn Service, Outdoor Detail, and the Headwaters Park Alliance work diligently each year to maintain the park professionally.

124

The park has also become the scene of a popular Christmas card with children playing in the snow. Cindie Rosswurm drew the picture for the card in 1995 to benefit the Turnstone Center for Disabled Children and Adults. The Headwaters Park Alliance reprinted the card in 2001 and sent it to friends and contributors.

Light the Fire Within

The 2002 Salt Lake Olympic Torch Relay is passing through Fort Wayne. Cheer on area torchbearers along the route or at any of the Rally Points. Then join us for a celebration at Headwaters Park for the Lighting of the Cauldron.

Salt Lake 2002 Olympic Torch Relay

Thursday, January 3, 2002

4:30 p.m.	Kick-off at Harding High School
5:00-8:00 p.m.	Rally Points along the route
	• Bishop Luers High School
	• Visitors Center/Convention & Visitors Bureau
	• Northside High School
	• Concordia High School
	• Glenbrook Square
	• Science Central
6:00-8:00 p.m.	Pre-celebration festivities with interactive exhibits, food and more at Headwaters Park
8:00 p.m.	Celebration at Hea...

A thrilling moment came on January 3, 2002, when the Olympic Torch was carried through Fort Wayne on its way to the winter games in Salt Lake City, Utah. The torch worked its way through the city, carried by dozens of relay runners, including Lizette Downey, seen here. The torch ended its journey in Headwaters Park with a ceremony and fireworks, enjoyed by over 10,000 people.

126

Pictured here is an aerial view of Headwaters Park, October 15, 1999.

www.ingramcontent.com/pod-product-compliance
Lightning Source LLC
Chambersburg PA
CBHW050631110426
42813CB00007B/1780